Dear Dad,
Saw this b   hday   r ot you!

                    jOY IT!!!

D1463173

GIL HODGES
THE QUIET MAN

GIL HODGES
THE QUIET MAN
By Marino Amoruso

Introduction by Pee Wee Reese

Paul S. Eriksson
PUBLISHER
MIDDLEBURY, VT 05753

Manufactured in the United States of America

10 9 8 7 6 5 4 3 2 1

Library of Congress Cataloging-in-Publication Data

Amoruso, Marino.
   Gil Hodges: the quiet man/by Marino Amoruso.
     p. cm.
   Includes index.
   ISBN 0-8397-2957-X: $19.95
   1. Hodges, Gil, 1924-1972. 2. Baseball players—United States-
-Biography. I. Title.
GV865.H57A48 1991
796.357'092—dc20
   [B]   91-3886
                                       CIP

Acknowledgments

Photo #'s 1, 2, 3, 5, 7, 12, 13, 14, 15, 16, 17, 18, 19, 21, 22, 23, 24, 25, 26, 27, 28, 31, 32, 33, 34, 35, 36, 37, 38, 39, 40, 41, 42 *courtesy of the National Baseball Hall of Fame Library.* Photo #'s 4, 20 *courtesy of the New York Mets.* Photo # 6 *courtesy of Ferd Richardson.* Photo # 8 *courtesy of Marjorie Hodges Maysent.* Photo #'s 9, 10, 46 *courtesy of Eddie & Roma Hawkins.* Photo # 45 *courtesy of Bill & Norma Thomas.* Photo #'s 11, 29, 30, 47, 48, 50 *courtesy of Dave Johnson.* Photo #'s 43, 44, 49, 52, 53 *by Marino Amoruso.* Photo # 51 *courtesy of the City of Petersburg, Indiana.*

To
my Aunt Phyllis Gallo
The most generous, kind, thoughtful,
giving person I've ever known.
I'll miss her always.

and to

The people of
Petersburg, Indiana

ONE OF THE MOST POPULAR MEN IN BASEBALL,
GIL EPITOMIZES THE COURAGE, SPORTSMANSHIP
AND INTEGRITY OF AMERICA'S FAVORITE PASTIME.

—Words on back of the Gil Hodges
1966 Topps baseball card.

Preface

This book is not a detailed biographical study. Rather, it is a tribute to, and a remembrance of, one of baseball's great men of character, Gil Hodges.

I researched this book by doing in-depth interviews with many of the people who knew Gil best, including his Brooklyn Dodger teammates, his friends, and the men he managed on the Washington Senators and New York Mets. Knowing the kind of man Gil Hodges was, I wasn't surprised to find that no one had anything negative to say about him. Yes, Gil Hodges had his faults, and yes, some of the men he played with and some he managed had their disagreements with him. But in reminiscing about Gil and their personal relationships with him, each person I spoke to remembered him only with respect, affection and warmth. This speaks volumes for the kind of man Gil Hodges was, and the way he touched the lives of those who knew him.

Gil Hodges was my first baseball hero and has always held a special place in my heart. I never saw Hodges play during his glory years with the Brooklyn Dodgers. I was one year old when Walter O'Malley moved the franchise from my hometown of Brooklyn to Los Angeles. My only recollections of Gil as a player are from 1962, when I was six years old and Gil was playing out the string with the expansion New York Mets. My father, however, had been a diehard Dodger fan and his favorite player had always been their big first baseman, Gil Hodges. When Gil came to the Mets in 1962 he immediately became my favorite. I had a Mets uniform with his number 14 sewn on the back, and on a rainy day in the early summer of 1962 I had the good fortune to meet him for a few moments. It remains one of my most cherished memories.

At first Gil became my hero simply because he was my father's hero. But as the years passed and I grew up, I came to understand the kind of man Gil was and my admiration for him grew. When he retired as an active player early in the 1963 season to manage the Washington Senators, I decided Washington would become my second favorite team after the Mets, and in this way I would still have a connection to Gil. He came home to manage the Mets in 1968, and in 1969 led them to one of the most remarkable and memorable World Championships in baseball history. It was, and will always remain, the most exciting baseball season I will ever know. My favorite team led to a World Championship by my boyhood idol. It was perfect. Absolutely perfect.

Much has been written about the 1969 New York Mets, but, surprisingly, few writers have taken the time to actually talk to the members of that historic team. It was my goal in writing about that season to have the players themselves tell most of the story, and I interviewed many of the 1969 Mets. The end result is, I hope, a unique and comprehensive behind-the-scenes account of that memorable year as told by the men who made it happen.

On April 2, 1972, a little over two years after leading the Mets to the top of the baseball world, Gil Hodges died of a heart attack at age 48 in West Palm Beach, Florida. A shy and modest man despite his many accomplishments on and off the field, Hodges probably would have been embarrassed by the tremendous outpouring of grief at his death.

Perhaps his Dodger teammate Pee Wee Reese summed up Hodges the man best when he told me: "You know, if you had a son, it would be a great thing to have him grow up to be just like Gil Hodges."

Introduction

Gil Hodges and I were teammates for fourteen years, first in Brooklyn and later in Los Angeles. During that time we went through quite a few ups and downs together. There were tight pennant races, glorious moments of victory, and more than a few heartbreaking losses. We won the National League Pennant in 1947, '49, '52 and '53, only to lose the World Series to the Yankees each time. We finally won it all in 1955. In the seventh game of that World Series we beat the Yankees 2 to 1. Gil Hodges drove in both of our runs. The last out of that game came when Elston Howard hit a ground ball to me at shortstop. My throw to first was a little low, but Gil scooped it up as he always did.

During my years with the Dodgers, we often played under enormous pressure. When Jackie Robinson joined the team in 1947 we became the focus of national attention. Yet we were able to win pennants and be a dominant team in our era. I am proud of that and of my teammates on that Brooklyn Dodger team who pulled together and played winning baseball despite the odds against us.

During those fourteen years when we played together—through the highs and lows of many baseball seasons—Gil was above all consistent, as a man and as a player. It didn't matter if the team was winning or losing, whether Gil himself was in a hot streak or in a horrendous slump, he was always a calming and reassuring presence on the field and in the clubhouse. On a team where emotions often ran high, Gil was a stabilizing influence.

I was the captain of the Brooklyn Dodgers but the team had many leaders. Gil Hodges was a man who led by example. In every inning of every game Gil ever played he gave his absolute best. He knew no other way to play, and he expected the same from his teammates. He was a man of high ideals who lived by them. The type of man who just commanded respect.

I know that on the inside Gil felt the same pressures, stress and emotions we all felt, but he never showed it. He was a man who kept everything inside. Maybe keeping all those emotions bottled up contributed to the heart attack that killed him at the age of forty-seven. He was such a physically strong man it is hard to believe he could die so young.

When Gil became a manager in 1963, it surprised many of us who knew him. There was no question he was a leader, that he knew the game as well as anybody, but Gil's quiet and subdued personality just didn't seem suited to managing in the big leagues. But he went on to become a great manager. In 1969 when he led his young New York Mets to that incredible World Championship, Gil Hodges was as resourceful and brilliant as any manager who ever skippered a big league team.

It was only a little more than two years after winning the World Series that Gil died. I saw him in Florida a few days before his heart attack. He looked healthy and strong, as he always did. It was so hard to accept the fact that the strongest one among us was the first to pass away.

Now, looking back at the years we spent together, many images of Gil come to mind. As a shortstop, looking across the diamond at Gil playing first base, I always had a feeling of great confidence. He was simply one of the finest defensive first basemen ever to play the game. He had enormous hands, and you knew that if you got the ball anywhere near him, he was going to catch it. He was a student of the game, and I can see him in the dugout studying the pitcher, looking for a weakness or a flaw he could use to his advantage. But as much as Gil loved baseball, and as dedicated as he was, it was not his first love. The most important thing in his life was his family. I think Gil himself would have preferred to be remembered as a good family man rather than as a ballplayer or a manager.

This tribute to Gil Hodges is long overdue. In his lifetime he never sought attention. Yet in his quiet way, he touched the lives of many thousands of people. Few ball players were more beloved or respected than Gil. I am proud to have been his teammate, and even prouder to have been his friend.

Pee Wee Reese

Contents

PART ONE

In the Rain at
the Polo Grounds

ONE

Gil, you're my favorite player

When the Dodgers left Brooklyn they took a piece of my father's heart with them. He had been a Dodger fan since he was a child in the early Thirties, and my grandfather had held season tickets for over three decades. As a youngster, my father would often cut school to go to Ebbets Field and watch the Dodgers play. While sitting in the bleachers he would hear this familiar voice booming across the ballpark. It was my grandfather, who had left work early to catch the Dodger game. Like father like son.

Together my old man and my grandfather suffered through the Thirties with a Dodger club known to all as the "Daffiness Boys" because of their losing antics on the field. Then came the pennant in 1941, followed by a loss to the Yankees in the World Series due in large part to Mickey Owen's infamous "missed third strike."

After the war came the glory years when the Brooklyn Dodgers became one of the greatest teams in the history of the game. With standout players such as Robinson, Snider, Campanella, Hodges and Reese, the Dodgers won the pennant six times in the 10–year span between 1947 and 1956. Unfortunately they lost the World Series to the hated Yankees in 1947, '49, '52, '53 and '56. But even these losses weren't as painful as the loss to the Giants in 1951, when Bobby Thomson hit his "shot heard 'round the world" against Ralph Branca in the third game of the pennant play-

3

offs. Of course, the play-offs were necessary only because the Dodgers blew a 16½–game lead they had held in mid-August. When Thomson's home run left the ball park, my grandfather put his foot through the radio on which he had been listening to the game.

Whenever the Dodgers lost in post-season play, the rallying cry of "Wait 'til Next Year" rose from the streets of Brooklyn. Unfortunately, in over 70 years of existence the Dodgers had never won a World Championship, and nobody was quite sure if and when "Next Year" would arrive.

Then, in 1955, it finally did come, and the Dodgers beat the Yankees in seven games to win Brooklyn's first and only World Championship. The city of Brooklyn had been waiting 75 years for such a victory, and at last it had come. That was the good news. The bad news was that two years later, in the winter of 1957, owner Walter O'Malley moved the club to Los Angeles.

Being Brooklyn Dodger fanatics, my grandfather and my father went through severe withdrawal pains when the team moved west. When the 1958 season opened they had no team to root for. Then, in the early summer of that year, my grandfather died. All in all it was not a banner year for my old man.

Without the Dodgers my father was in absolute baseball limbo, as was the entire borough of Brooklyn. Obviously he couldn't root for the Yankees; that would have been sacrilegious. So, in order to satisfy his craving for baseball, my father watched the Yankees and rooted for whatever team they were playing against.

My earliest memories of baseball are from 1960. I was four years old, and my father and I sat in the living room of our house in Flatbush watching the Yankees and rooting against them. It seemed strange to me that we didn't have a favorite team. When you're a kid it's important to have a favorite player, but I didn't even have a favorite team. Like my old man, I just rooted for the entire American League against the Yankees.

We didn't watch the game too closely anyway. Usually my father spent the entire time telling me about the Brooklyn Dodgers. I learned that Jackie Robinson was the most exciting player my father had ever seen, and that he was the first Negro to play in the major leagues. "You should have seen Jackie steal home," my father would say with fire in his eyes. "Nobody could shake up a pitcher like Robinson. He'd dance off third base and just taunt the pitcher. Then he'd take off and slide home safely in a cloud of dust. You should have seen it!"

I learned about Carl Furillo's cannon arm, and how he played the right-field wall at Ebbets Field so well. I also came to understand that Furillo held a special place in my grandfather's heart because he was a fellow Italian. I heard about catcher Roy Campanella's monstrous blasts, and the way captain Pee Wee Reese scooped them up at shortstop. I knew that Duke Snider played a graceful and stylish center field, and that Carl Erskine had a wicked curveball.

But of all the Dodgers my old man spoke about, his favorite was the big first baseman, Gil Hodges. My father told me what a fine fielder he was, and that he had tremendous hands. I was told of Gil's awesome power from the right side of the plate, and that he wore number 14. But above all my father stressed that Gil Hodges was a real gentleman, a man to be admired for the way he conducted himself on the field and off.

By the age of five I probably knew more about the Brooklyn Dodgers than any other child in the Free World. Even though they no longer played in Brooklyn, they became my favorite team. To me the Brooklyn Dodgers were mythical legends of the past. Whenever I played stoopball with my friends I made believe I was Carl Furillo or Duke Snider or Gil Hodges, although I had never seen any of them play.

One day while playing stoopball I proudly announced that I was going to be Jackie Robinson. Some teenager sitting on the stoop next door told me I couldn't be Jackie Robinson.

"Why not?" I asked him.

"Because Jackie Robinson is a nigger," he said.

I had no idea what he was talking about. I had never heard the expression "nigger" before. That night at dinner, just as my old man was about to put a forkful of baked zitis in his mouth, I asked him, "Dad, is Jackie Robinson a nigger?"

The fork stopped about an inch from his mouth. He looked over at my mother, then at me. "Where did you hear that?" he asked.

"Some kid said I couldn't be Jackie Robinson because he's a nigger."

My old man looked at my mother again, then at my two-year-old kid brother, who was having difficulty getting a fistful of zitis into his mouth. My old man put down his fork. "That is a very bad word," he said. "You are never to use it again. If I ever hear you say that word again you're going to be punished. Do you understand?"

I nodded; "But what does it mean?"

"It's a very bad word that stupid people use when they're talking about a Negro. We don't use that word." He paused, and knowing my admiration of the mythical and legendary Brooklyn Dodgers, added: "None of the Dodgers would ever use that word, because Jackie Robinson was their teammate and friend. I don't ever want to hear that word come out of your mouth again. Do you understand?"

"Yes sir."

My lessons in the legend, lore and history of the Brooklyn Dodgers continued through the 1960 and '61 baseball seasons. We still watched the Yankees and rooted against them, but somehow I felt deprived. It was a very difficult thing to have a favorite team that you couldn't watch play because they no longer existed. I began to regret that I had been born too late to have seen the Dodgers play in Brooklyn.

Then, in the spring of 1962, a miracle occurred. The New York Mets were born and National League baseball was coming back to New York. At last my old man and I had a team of our own, one that we could actually watch play. Even more exciting was the fact that this new team had acquired the services of Gil Hodges to play first base. Because he was my father's favorite player and because he was a Met, Gil Hodges became the first true hero of my life.

The 1962 Mets were perhaps the worst team in the history of baseball. In their first year they won only 42 games and lost the staggering total of 120. But to me it just didn't matter. I thought they were the greatest ball club ever assembled.

My father and I would watch their games on TV every night. Unfortunately my bed time arrived around the third or fourth inning, so I didn't see many completed games. Because of this a ritual started around my house. Every morning my father got up to go to work about five o'clock. From my room I would hear him get out of bed and go into the bathroom. I'd get up, walk to the bathroom door and knock. From inside the bathroom, above the running water, I'd hear my old man say, "They lost." This ritual hardly ever varied. On the few occasions when he replied with "They won," it was difficult for me to get back to sleep because of my excitement.

Gil Hodges played only 54 games for the Mets in 1962. He was 38 years old, far past his prime, and his legs were giving out. But at six I wasn't aware that a ballplayer could be past his prime, or that an injury could keep him out of the lineup. All I knew was that Gil Hodges was my idol and that I wanted to be a first baseman.

Around mid-July in 1962 my father came home from work one day with two packages. I didn't think much about it until he handed them to me. In one was a first baseman's glove, and in the other a Mets uniform with a big, blue number 14 sewn on the back. To say that I was beside myself with excitement would be an understatement. But there was more. My old man told me to put on the uniform because we were going to the Polo Grounds to watch the Mets play.

As soon as we got in the car it started to rain. It came down in buckets. My father seemed perturbed, but the thought of a rainout never entered my mind. All I was thinking was that it was taking an awful long time to get to the ball park. Every five minutes I asked the old man if we were almost there. And each time he answered me with, "Almost."

When we arrived at the Polo Grounds the rain had turned into a light drizzle. My father grabbed my right hand (the first baseman's glove was on my left) and led me toward the entrance. I was absolutely in awe at the size of the place, and all the people streaming toward it. The entire experience seemed like a dream. I walked as fast as I could because I had this irrational fear that I'd wake up from this wonderful dream.

Our first stop inside the Polo Grounds was at the souvenir stand. My father bought me a yearbook, a program, a Mets doll with a bobbing head, a Mets hat, a Mets pennant and a Mets pen and pencil set in the shape of bats.

Taking my hand, my old man started to walk toward the ramp that led to the section where our seats were. We walked into the darkness of the tunnel and emerged into the brightness and noise of the stadium. The thing I remember most clearly from that magical moment were the vivid colors—the deep green of the grass; the brown of the infield dirt and pitcher's mound; the blue, orange and bright white of the Met uniforms; the gray and blue of the Chicago Cub uniforms. It was breathtaking; one of those moment of pure happiness that happen so rarely in life. Every Mets game I had seen up to that point had been on our black and white Motorola television set, and I guess I had never realized how colorful a ball park was. I also remember the sharp crack of the bat as the Mets took batting practice. I was hooked. To this day, almost three decades later, I still get that same magical feeling whenever I walk up a ramp into a ball park.

An usher showed us to our seats, which were on the first-base side, field level, about 20 rows back. I put down my armful of souvenirs on the seat and scanned the field for Gil Hodges. I spotted him standing near the batting cage. I couldn't believe it. There he was, number 14, standing maybe 50 yards from me. I tapped my old man on the shoulder and pointed. My father nodded, smiled and said, "Look at the size of his arms." They were big. Gil Hodges was big; bigger than life to me.

Then it started to rain again. It rained heavily. The players ran for cover into the dugout, and everybody seated on the field level of the Polo Grounds ran for cover underneath the loge section. The grounds crew put the tarp on the field, and at that moment it suddenly dawned on me that my first big league game might very possibly be rained out. I started crying. I don't think to this day I've ever had a more desperate feeling of disappointment than I did when that tarp went on the field.

My old man squatted down next to me. "Don't worry," he said as he took out his handkerchief and wiped my face, "It'll stop." And 20 minutes later it did. The players came back on the field and the fans back into the field-level seats.

My father and I, however, did not go back to our seats. He took my hand and we walked straight toward the field, just to the left of the Mets dugout. About 10 rows from the field an usher was diverting people who were trying to reach the railing. This didn't seem to discourage my old man. We just kept walking.

A big smile crossed the usher's face as we approached. He and my old man shook hands. It turned out that they knew each other from Ebbets Field days. They spoke for a few moments. The usher was sorry to hear that my grandfather had passed away. They shook hands again and we were allowed to pass. A moment later my father and I were standing by the railing about 20 feet to the left of the Mets dugout. Again I searched the field for Gil Hodges, only this time I couldn't find him. Most of the other Mets were out there, but not Gil. My disappointment was tempered by the fact that I was only a few feet away from my other Met heroes. Players like Jay Hook, Elio Chicon, Charlie Neal, Marv Throneberry, Frank Thomas and many more of the players who made up the most hapless team in modern baseball history.

With my Mets uniform on I felt like part of the team. I was hoping they would notice that I was wearing it. With my yearbook clutched in my right hand, and a pen in my left. I was about to be introduced to the wonderful pastime of collecting autographs.

Jay Hook was the first player to come over. He started about 15 feet to my right and worked his way down the railing, signing autographs as he went. In the next 20 minutes or so, almost every Met player came over to sign. My yearbook was filled with their signatures. All except that of Gil Hodges.

The Mets finished batting practice and the Cubs took over. All the Met players left the field except for the coaches and manager Casey Stengel, who was standing in front of the dugout eating an ice cream cone.

I stared at Casey for a moment or two and then glanced over to my right toward the Mets dugout. A second later Gil Hodges emerged. He came over to the railing and began signing autographs. He was working his way toward me. Again I tapped my old man and pointed. "He'll be here in a few seconds," he said.

I couldn't believe what was happening. In just a few short moments I would be meeting Gil Hodges. He would be standing in front of me. He'd talk to me. Meeting a baseball idol is without question the single greatest experience a six-year-old can have. And it was about to happen to me.

Unfortunately I was faced with what seemed at the time a horrible dilemma. Should I stand facing the field to meet Gil face to face, or should I turn around so he could see the number 14 on my back? It was very important to me that Gil Hodges know he was my favorite player. I could tell him this, of course, but I was sure he would be much more impressed if he saw the number 14 on the back of my uniform.

Gil was getting closer and I was in an absolute quandary. Suddenly I felt my feet leave the ground. My old man solved my problem by picking me up and seating me on the railing with my back toward the field. "Let Gil see the number 14 on your uniform," he said.

I felt my father's hands tighten on my shoulders, then I heard a voice say, "Well, it's number 14; must be Gil Hodges."

My old man picked me up off the railing, turned me around, and there was Gil Hodges. Standing right there in front of me. I have tried over the years to describe to people my feelings when I saw Gil Hodges standing before me, but how can you possibly put into words the emotions of a small child whose most fervent wish and dream is coming true before his eyes? I wasn't looking at his picture in the yearbook. I wasn't looking at his baseball card. I wasn't seeing him on TV. He was standing right there, talking to me, smiling at me.

To my amazement I found it impossible to speak.

"What's your name?" Gil asked.

I opened my mouth but nothing came out, so my old man answered for me.

"How old are you?" Gil asked, and again my vocal abilities proved useless.

"He's six," my father said.

"Well," said Gil, "you're a big guy for your age."

My mind was racing. Gil Hodges had just told me I was a big guy. Compared to him I was a midget. He stood there towering over me with a warm smile on his face. His arms were enormous; they seemed to bulge from his shirt.

Looking back at that day, I know now that Gil Hodges must have known just how nervous I was. I'm sure he had met thousands of children who had the same reaction. Just stunned silence.

Gil reached over the railing and gently took the yearbook and pen from my hand. He leafed through the yearbook until he found his picture, looked up at me and then at my father. The old man told him how to spell my name and Gil signed the page while I thought what a dope I had been for not having the yearbook opened to Gil's page.

Gil handed the yearbook and pen back to me. Then he bent down a little to be more on my level and said, "You keep practicing and maybe someday you'll be out here on the field wearing number 14." Then he reached over the railing and shook my hand, my six-year-old paw completely disappearing into his huge right hand.

An alarm went off in my mind. Gil Hodges was standing in front of me. It was a moment I had always dreamed about, and I hadn't said one word to him. Not one word. I had played this scene many times in my head, and each time Gil and I had long conversations. But now it was actually happening and I just stood there with my mouth hanging open.

Suddenly I was gripped by fear. I came to the sobering realization that if I didn't say something at that moment I might never get another chance. He was looking right into my eyes. He was smiling at me. He had bent down to get closer to me. I wanted to say something, anything, but I didn't know what to say. My mind was a blank.

Then I heard a voice. It was my voice, and it was saying, "Gil, you're my favorite player."

Gil smiled a little wider, put his hand on my shoulder and said, "And you're my favorite fan."

At that moment I reached the highest plateau any six-year-old baseball fan can possibly reach. My idol, my favorite player, had told me that I was his favorite fan. I hadn't thought ballplayers had favorite fans the way fans have favorite ballplayers. Obviously I was wrong because Gil Hodges had just told me I was his favorite fan.

"I have to go now," Gil said; "But you remember to be good and always listen to your parents." He smiled at my father and then looked down at me. Again he took my hand and shook it.

I watched him as he walked toward the dugout. The fans on the railing were calling his name and Gil smiled and waved to them. Then he went down the dugout steps.

A few minutes later the Cubs finished batting practice and it started to pour again. Players from each dugout raced toward the center-field fence which opened up and led to the clubhouses at the old Polo Grounds. I watched Gil Hodges trot toward center field. I didn't care if the game was rained out. It didn't seem important anymore. At that moment, standing in the rain at the Polo Grounds, I was absolutely contented with my life. It was a feeling I haven't had since that day all those years ago.

rooklyn's slugging first baseman, Gil Hodges, in 1952, during the prime of his
reer.

The legendary Brooklyn Dodgers of the 1950s. *From left to right;* Pee Wee Reese
Carl Furillo, Jackie Robinson, Carl Erskine, Gil Hodges, Don Newcombe and Ro
Campanella.

Gil Hodges as a Los Angeles Dodger in 1961, his last year with the organization. In 1962 he would come home to New York as a member of the Mets.

Gil as a member of the expansion New York Mets in 1962. He appeared in only 5?
games that year, but hit the first home run in the club's history.

ove: Gil holds the bat
l ball with which he hit
370th and last major
gue home run. August
l, 1962.

with another baseball
end, Casey Stengel,
nager of the 1962
zinal Mets.

Gil in early 1963. He would retire 11 games into the season to become the manager of the Washington Senators.

PART TWO

Character, Dignity, Courage

TWO

Go home, keep the commandments,
and say a prayer for Gil Hodges

In the 1952 World Series Gil Hodges came to the plate 26 times. He walked five times but went hitless in his other 21 attempts. A powerful weapon in the awesome Brooklyn Dodger attack, Hodges was humbled by Yankee pitching. Although he went hitless through seven games and the Yankees beat the Dodgers for the fourth straight time in Series play, not once did Gil hear a boo or a catcall from the crowd. Instead, they cheered him louder and louder each time he came to bat.

The slump continued through the early part of the 1953 season. By the middle of May Gil was hitting an anemic .187. Still he heard nothing but cheers from the Ebbets Field faithful. Each week he received hundreds of letters and telegrams wishing him luck and offering advice. His locker was filled with good luck charms sent by concerned fans everywhere. Concern welled up from the streets of Brooklyn to support Hodges through his prolonged slump.

"The fans started sending me letters telling me they were praying for me," recalled Gil of this period of his career. "Some of them said they were making novenas for me. Others said they are saying the Rosary for me during the game. Some kids wrote that they were going to Mass for me every morning before they went to school. I even got a letter from two nuns in Pittsburgh who told me not to give up;

they're saying prayers for my special intention in their convent every day."

On a hot Sunday in late May of 1953, Father Herbert Redmond addressed his congregation at the St. Francis Xavier Roman Catholic Church in Brooklyn. "It's too hot for a sermon today," he told them. "Go home, keep the commandments, and say a prayer for Gil Hodges." Father Redmond's words reflected the feelings of all Brooklyn Dodger fans. They loved the slugger and suffered with him as he struggled at the plate.

Even Ty Cobb, who has been described as "mean, vindictive, selfish, vain, [and] cruel," got into the act. Writing Hodges that he had "been in deep water myself and no one to help me," Cobb offered to correspond with Hodges about fundamentals, stipulating only that there be "no publicity crediting me."

The slump became so bad that Dodger manager Charlie Dressen finally benched Hodges. "Maybe you're just trying too hard," Dressen told Gil. The big first baseman rode the bench for five games. Then Dressen sent him in to pinch hit in a game against the Giants at the Polo Grounds. Gil lined a solid single to left field off Dave Koslo. As Gil rounded first the Giant fans gave him a rousing ovation.

Gil was back in the starting lineup the next day, but went hitless in his first two games. Then, in the following two games against Philadelphia, Hodges got five hits. The slump was over. He finished the year with a .302 average, 31 homers and 122 RBIs. In the 1953 World Series he led the Dodgers in hitting with a .365 mark, and in 1954 he had the best year of his career, hitting .304 with 42 home runs and 130 RBIs. The next season, 1955, the Brooklyn Dodgers won their first and only World championship, with Gil delivering the game-winning hit in the seventh contest.

Across 18 major league seasons Gil Hodges hit a solid .273 and blasted 370 home runs. He hit over 20 home runs in 11 seasons, topping the 30 mark six times and the 40 mark twice. He walloped 14 grand slams, placing him third on the all-time list, and is one of only nine players in big league history to launch four round-trippers in a single game. He was also a clutch hitter, knocking in more than 100 runs in seven consecutive seasons from 1949 to 1955; and he was durable, playing in over 100 games for 14 straight seasons between 1948 and 1961. One of the greatest defensive first basemen in the game's history, he was selected to the National League All-Star team eight times.

As a big league manager, Hodges led the 1969 New York Mets to what was perhaps the most exciting and remarkable World Championship our national game has ever known. It was a World Championship that lifted the spirits of an entire nation, and it came at a time when America sorely needed its spirits lifted.

But for all his heroics on the ball field, perhaps Gil's finest hours in baseball came during his slump of the 1952 World Series and early 1953 season. It was a time of frustration and misery for Hodges, but the fans stuck by him and proved how much they loved him.

Baseball fans loved Hodges for more than his formidable abilities on a baseball diamond. They knew that although he was a large and powerful man, it was inner strength that motivated the big first baseman. He was a man of high ideals, of great character, dignity and courage. In moments of success and triumph he was modest and reserved. In times of trouble and failure he was a calming and reassuring force. He held a special place in the hearts of fans and players alike. In many ways he typified the American hero of a bygone era—a man of action and few words. In the excitement, chaos and emotional roller coaster that was Ebbets Field in the Fifties, Gil Hodges was sea of calm, at least on the surface.

Strong, reserved, soft-spoken and always a true gentleman, Gil was also a stoic man. Whatever pain, frustration, anger, aggravation or pressure he felt he bore silently and battled against within himself. He rarely vented stress through emotional outburst. It wasn't Gil's way. He believed a man dealt with his own problems and fought his own battles. A man lived up to the responsibilities he had taken on. He took care of his family and friends. He understood what the priorities in life were, the important things. He paid for his mistakes by himself, and shared his successes with others. A man was modest about his triumphs, knowing that failure is far more frequent in this life than is success. A man took everything in stride, with humility, grace, modesty and dignity.

This was the credo Gil Hodges lived by every day of his life. It wasn't always easy, but he never faltered in his beliefs. In the pressure cooker that is big league baseball, especially big league baseball in New York City, it is doubly difficult to live by these standards. But Gil always stood by what he believed in. The stress and pressure of eighteen years as a big league player and nine as a manager stayed locked within him. It is ironic that many of the qualities for which Hodges was admired and loved were also personality characteristics that in some measure contributed to his early heart disease.

"He was a quiet strength on the field and in the clubhouse," remembers pitcher Carl Erskine, Gil's Dodger teammate for 12 years. "His presence was always felt even though he wasn't a holler guy. I can remember that he'd walk to the mound in a tight situation, and he didn't have a whole lot to say, but whatever he did say was right to the heart of the matter. Just his being out there gave you strength. It gave you confidence."

"A silent leader" is how Brooklyn relief ace Clem Labine remembers Gil. "He was the quiet man, a great silent strength. I always felt Gilly was someone I could turn to and rely on. He was sort of a father figure on the club."

"When I think of Gil Hodges I think of a perfect gentleman," says Preacher Roe, Gil's fellow Dodger for seven seasons. "I liked Gil so much. He was such a fine man. He was kind, good-natured, very mild and very intelligent. I just couldn't believe it when he passed away," Roe continues, shaking his head sadly. "I always thought that there was a man who was going to live forever. He was so strong, so healthy. And then back in '72 when I read that his heart gave out on him . . . Jeez, I just couldn't believe it. . . . He was only 47 years old."

"The irony of life, and in this case, of our team," says Carl Erskine, "is that the two strongest men on the field, Gil Hodges and Jackie Robinson, were the first to have these serious health problems that resulted in their death. . . . You know, I went to Gil's father's funeral in Petersburg some years ago, and his father died exactly the way Gil did; his heart gave out on him. Then Gil died, and after his death his older brother Bob died from a massive heart attack as well. Afterwards, whenever I happened to be going down Highway 57 here in Indiana, I always stopped by to see Gil's mom out in Petersburg. She lost all three of her boys in the same way."

"Baseball lost one of its greatest men when Gil died," says Hall of Fame pitcher Don Drysdale, who roomed with Gil on the road for six years. "You know, it's a funny thing. I talk baseball with hundreds of people—players, coaches, managers, fans, executives—and whenever Gil's name comes up in conversation everybody becomes quiet and listens closely. It's really an interesting thing to see. The absolute respect everybody has for this man. And when people talk about Gil, people who knew him, they speak with a respect, reverence and emotion that's different from the way they talk about anybody else. It always makes me smile when I see that. I was very lucky to have known Gil, to have been his roommate when I was a young player. He taught me how to be a big leaguer. I guess everybody who knew him was lucky. He was just a great human being. My life is greater because of him, having known him.

*   *   *

GILBERT RAYMOND HODGES WAS BORN ON APRIL 4, 1924, in Princeton, Indiana. When he was seven, his family moved to Petersburg, about 30 miles to the north. Located in the southwest corner of the state, Petersburg is coal country. To support the Hodges family Gil's father, Charlie, spent his working adult life in the dark, damp, suffocating coal mines. When his sons, Bob and "Bud," as Gil was known to his friends and family, reached the age when they too could work in the mines, big Charlie Hodges wouldn't hear of it. "No," he told them. "Not my sons. I've spent my life in those mines; that's enough. You can work around the mines . . . above ground."

The senior Hodges was a physically powerful man, as his sons would be, but he knew how a life in the mines could kill a man piece by piece. Charlie Hodges had been in three mine accidents during his lifetime, resulting in the loss of an eye and some toes. The black coal dust he inhaled every day clogged his lungs and made it difficult to breathe. Often his whole body trembled and shook with coughing fits. No, Charlie Hodges decided very early on, his sons would not travel down into the earth as he had done. There had to be another way. Charlie himself never had the chance to get out of the mines, but he would make sure his sons did.

It was in the fall of 1952, the end of Gil's fifth season as a Brooklyn Dodger, when Charlie Hodges was involved in yet another mine accident. This time he would not recover.

A heavy load of coal shale fell on his legs, injuring his right knee. It was not a serious injury, but Gil persuaded his father to have minor surgery done to correct the problem. The doctors said surgery wasn't absolutely necessary, but Gil compared it to the trick knee ballplayers sometimes get and urged his father to check into the hospital.

The surgery was performed and Charlie Hodges was in fine spirits. But while he lay in bed recovering, a blood clot formed in his leg and raced to his heart, killing the big man instantly. He was only 54 years old.

"It was in the off-season then," recalled Gil of his father's death, "and I was lolling around the house enjoying the luxury of being with my wife, Joan, and our kids, and taking the kids to school every morning. Every weekend I planned to go out to Indiana and see my father and mother, and every weekend I kept putting it off. I telephoned, sure, but it wasn't like being there with them.

"With the first surge of grief I felt on my father's death I felt a deep remorse. I was the one who talked him into getting the operation, The doctors said it really wouldn't have made any difference. But if I had gone home I would have been there when it happened. Why wasn't I there? Now it was too late. During the 900-mile drive from Brooklyn to Indiana I kept thinking I could have been a more dutiful son. I kept thinking a lot of other things, too."

One of the things Gil thought about on his drive home was how his father had spent as many hours as he could teaching his sons to play ball. Both boys were natural athletes, big, strong and well-coordinated like their father. Bob, 14 months Gil's senior, was considered the real pro prospect in the family. He signed a Class D contract as a pitcher with the Detroit Tigers organization in 1941, but a dead arm ended his career before the year was out.

Gil was more of an all-around athlete than his brother, starring in baseball, football, basketball and track while in high school. When he graduated in 1941, he too was offered a Class D contract by the Tigers; but he turned it down, opting to attend St. Joseph's College on an athletic scholarship. "I was offered a chance to go to St. Joseph's near home," recalled Gil, "and even though I was crazy about playing ball, I thought going to college was a little more sensible. Besides, I had ideas about becoming a college coach someday, and everybody said the physical education course at St. Joe's was a good one. So I accepted the scholarship, and off I went."

Gil attended St. Joseph's for two years, lettering in baseball, football, basketball and track. During summer vacations, he played ball in the industrial leagues around Indianapolis. It was in the summer of 1943 that Stanley Feezle, a local sporting goods dealer and part-time Dodger scout, spotted Gil. Feezle convinced the 19-year-old Hodges to go

with him to a Dodger tryout camp in Olean, New York. Jake
Pitler, the manager of the Dodgers' farm club in Olean, was
so impressed with the 6'1" 200-pound youngster that he
phoned Dodger president Branch Rickey and urged him to
sign Hodges immediately. "He's one in a million," said
Pitler. "Don't let him get away."

Gil then traveled to Brooklyn to work out under the
watchful eye of Branch Rickey himself at Ebbets Field. After
playing him at every position except pitcher, Rickey signed
Gil as a catcher for a $500 bonus. It was one of the best
bargains Rickey ever got.

Gil played in one game for the Dodgers in August of 1943,
as a third baseman. Facing the Cincinnati Reds and Johnny
Vander Meer, Gil walked, stole a base and struck out twice. A
short time later World War II beckoned and Gil, a member of
the Marine R.O.T.C. program, was called into active service.

Gil spent the next two years in the Marines as a gunner for
the 16th Anti-Aircraft Battalion. For 18 months he was sta-
tioned in the South Pacific, and saw battle action on Iwo
Jima and Okinawa. But this was a period of his life which Gil
never spoke about, and deeds he performed on those bloody
Pacific battlefields remained untold.

"In all the years we played together, I never heard him
mention his time in the service once," recalls Carl Erskine.
"It was something he just didn't talk about."

"He never talked about his time in the Marines," says
attorney Sid Loberfeld, Gil's close friend and business associ-
ate for over 26 years. "But I'll tell you one thing, every year
the Marines hold a dinner in his honor and give an award in
his name because they know what kind of man he was."

"I was in the Marines, too," says Carl Furillo, Gil's roommate for 10 seasons, "but we never really talked about it in
all the time we spent together. Every once in a while I'd say
something general about it or he would, but never a whole
lot. That's just the way it was with Gil."

The only aspect of his military career that Gil spoke about
was the fact that he took up smoking cigarettes "to have
something to do sitting in those holes in Okinawa."

Gil's Marine background surfaced dramatically a week after his young Mets won the 1969 World Series. On October 25, 1969, the first issue of a magazine called *Jock* hit the newsstands. Its cover featured a photo of models portraying the Mets planting the World Championship flag on the mound at Shea Stadium. The models were depicted in the exact pose of the men in the world-famous photo of the Marines planting the American flag on Iwo Jima's Mount Suribachi. The cover offended Gil. He had been on Iwo Jima. He had seen thousands of American boys die in the brutal battles for possession of that remote Pacific island. "Nobody is prouder of my players than I am," said Gil after seeing the magazine cover, "but they just won a baseball championship. The boys they are mocking in this picture died for their country."

When Gil was discharged from the Marines in the winter of 1945, Branch Rickey gave him another $500 bonus and sent him to the Dodger farm club in Newport News to learn the fine art of catching.

In the off-season during his first two years out of the service, Gil returned home to Indiana to attend Oakland City College on the G.I. bill and get his degree. While there he played varsity basketball. "He was the best-known athlete we ever had," said Oakland City basketball coach Delbert Disler. "I think he could have played pro basketball if he'd wanted to."

Gil earned a spot on the Brooklyn Dodgers in the spring of 1947 as a third-string catcher behind Bruce Edwards and Bobby Bragan, and saw action in only 28 games. The following year Dodger skipper Leo Durocher made a move that would have a profound impact on both Hodges and the Dodgers. During the off-season second baseman Eddie Stanky had been traded to the Boston Braves. So, for 1948, Durocher moved Jackie Robinson from first base to his natural position at second, called up a hard-hitting young catcher named Roy Campanella from the Dodgers' farm team in St. Paul-Minneapolis, and installed Hodges at first base. Gil had never played the position before, but he worked hard at it and with his big, capable hands he was soon handling it as if he had played there his whole life. He went on to become one of the best-fielding first basemen the game has ever known. "He had great footwork and it enabled him to come off the bag a fraction of a second sooner than he probably should have," recalls Carl Erskine. "Boy, he'd steal so many plays for us at first like that. It used to drive the other managers up the wall. And Gil had great hands. Anything he could get to you can be sure Gil grabbed."

"He was the best I ever saw defensively at first base," says Brooklyn Hall-of-Fame shortstop Pee Wee Reese. "He had those big hands and he could just scoop anything up. If I had to go in the hole to get a ball and I threw the ball in the dirt, Gil would just dig it out with those big hands and save me. You always knew that Gil was going to come up with the ball and it made you more relaxed and at ease out there."

"Gil made everything look easy at first base," says Carl Furillo. "He was so smooth that even the hard plays looked easy when Gil made them. In all my years in baseball I never saw a better first baseman than Gil."

"We used to marvel at the way Gil could play defense," remembers Brooklyn's great center fielder Duke Snider. "Any throw that went over to first base you knew Gil was going to come up with. In fact, he was so steady that if he didn't come up with a throw it made you wonder if he wasn't feeling well that day."

Gil's hands were huge but "soft," as ballplayers term a good pair of hands. "Gil wears a glove at first only because it's fashionable," Pee Wee Reese often joked. "With those hands he really doesn't need one."

Although he was consistently excellent in the field, Gil was a streaky hitter, either very hot or very cold. But his offense never affected his defense. "Quite often a player reflects his poor offensive performance by beginning to crack on defense," observes Clem Labine. "Not Gilly. I don't think we ever saw Gil in what can be considered a defensive slump. He had some prolonged slumps at the plate, but it never affected him in the field."

In addition to his defensive prowess, Gil's physical strength was legendary. One time a writer commented to Leo Durocher on the strength of Reds slugger Ted Kluszewski. "Klu?" said Leo; "He's strong, but not Hodges strong." Leo pounded the dugout roof: "Concrete; that's Gil, concrete."

"Oh, Lord, was he a strong man," remembers Brooklyn Dodger Hall-of-Fame catcher Roy Campanella. "He was the most powerful man in baseball. But Gil was such a quiet and gentle man, he'd never use his strength to hurt anybody. It just wasn't his way."

Because of his size and strength, Hodges could have intimidated anybody in baseball had he chosen to do so. But he never did. Dodger skipper Charlie Dressen once offered Gil a cash bonus if he would lose his cool, argue with an umpire about a close play, and get ejected from the game. Gil refused to do it. "That's not my style," he told Dressen, "but thanks anyway."

When a fight broke out on the field, Gil used his enormous strength to stop it. "He was the biggest and strongest guy out there," says Preacher Roe, "but he was always the guy breaking up the fight."

The most legendary example of Gil's peacemaking took place at Ebbets Field in the summer of 1957. The Dodgers were playing the Braves, and the Braves' Johnny Logan started a fist fight with Brooklyn hurler Don Drysdale. It seems Logan felt that the big right-hander had purposely thrown at him. (Drysdale was famous for his "purpose pitches," so Logan, in all likelihood, had a legitimate gripe.) Soon after Logan and Drysdale tangled, Braves third baseman Eddie Mathews jumped on Drysdale's back and began swinging at him. The three tumbled to the ground as the other players on the field joined in the fracas.

At this point Gil calmly walked over to the tangle of players on the mound, reached in, and, grabbing Mathews by the foot, dragged him across the infield to the Braves' dugout. "Here," said Gil to the startled Braves, "where shall I deposit him?"

"I remember that incident," says Don Drysdale with a chuckle. "Everybody on the field was just amazed. I mean, Eddie Mathews was a big guy, a real strong guy. But Gil just dragged him to the Braves' dugout like it was nothing. That will give you an idea how strong Gil was.

"I remember another time when I was just amazed at Gil's strength. We were on the road in St. Louis, staying at the old Chase Hotel. So after the game we go up to our room, Gil and I, and we both had those big old suitcases. They were about nine or 10 inches wide across the top, and packed with all our clothes for the road trip. Well, we tried to open the door and it jammed, like it was stuck on something, and we could only get it open a few inches. So Gil gives the door a shove and wedges his body in. Then, Gil just palmed the suitcases like a basketball. I mean he just put one hand over the top of his suitcase, picked it up and threw it in the room. Then he picked up mine and threw that in the room. Needless to say I was amazed at his strength. My eyes were as wide as saucers. Then we both squeezed into the room and Gil turns to me and smiles and says, 'Roomie, I'm hungry. Let's order a couple of those brownie □a-la-modes from room service.' "

In keeping with his quiet and reserved personality, Gil had a very dry sense of humor. One Friday night, while flying home to Brooklyn from a road trip, the in-flight meal featured steak as the main course. Being a devout Catholic, Gil would not eat it. A teammate pointed out to him that under such conditions an automatic dispensation was allowed. "I know," smiled Gil as he looked out the window at the sky, "but we're just a little bit too close to headquarters up here."

"Gil had a real good sense of humor and a keen insight into people," recalls Frank Howard, who played with him on the Los Angeles Dodgers, as well as playing under him when Gil managed the Washington Senators. "He could needle with the best of them, but in a very dry, understated way. But he always made his point."

THE BROOKLYN DODGER TEAM THAT HODGES PLAYED for from 1947 to 1957, when the franchise moved to Los Angeles, was not only one of the greatest clubs ever assembled, but also one of the most popular and best-loved teams in baseball history. As Roger Kahn wrote in his classic book *The Boys of Summer,* "A whole country was stirred by the high deeds and thwarted longings of the Duke, Preacher, Pee Wee, Skoonj and the rest. Their skills lifted everyman's spirit and their defeat joined them with everyman's existence, a national team, with a country in thrall, irresistible and unable to beat the Yankees."

Indeed the Dodger-Yankee post-season confrontations represented the classic American rivalry: the underdog Dodgers, team of the masses, against the mighty, affluent New York Yankees. And the damn Yankees always won.

The Dodger-Yankee World Series pattern had been set in 1941 with the first meeting of the two teams. The Bombers took the Bums in five games, and the turning point of that Series was, of course, catcher Mickey Owen's infamous "missed third strike" in the fourth game. At the time the Yankees led the Series two games to one, but the Dodgers led the fourth contest—played at Ebbets Field—by the score of 4–3 with two gone and none on in the ninth. Brooklyn hurler Hugh Casey got two quick strikes on Yankee batsman Tommy Henrich, and the Bums were just one strike away from tying the Series. On the next pitch Casey broke off a tremendous curveball (some say spitball) that completely fooled Henrich, who swung and missed for strike three. Unfortunately for the Dodgers, catcher Mickey Owen was also completely fooled by the pitch, and as it rolled to the backstop Henrich made first base easily. It was all the Yankees needed as they exploded for four runs to defeat the Dodgers 7–4. After the game Henrich felt some sympathy for Owen, saying: "That was a tough break; I bet Owen feels like a nickel's worth of dog meat."

The next day the entire borough of Brooklyn felt "like a nickel's worth of dog meat" when the Yankees beat a deflated Dodger club to take the title. And so the Brooklyn Dodger tradition of losing to the Yankees in the World Series was born.

This tradition continued in the post-war years as the Yankees beat the Dodgers in the 1947, '49, '52 and '53 World Series. All of these fall confrontations were incredibly exciting; all featured plays that would live forever in the legend, lore and history of the game; and all ended with the Yankees emerging victorious.

"We were beginning to wonder if we were ever going to beat the Yankees," recalls Duke Snider. "The Yankees weren't better than us. I'm not saying we were better, but we felt we were just as good. It was just one of those things. We couldn't win the odd game. We needed someone or something to push us over that final hump to win the Series."

Of course the Dodgers' several defeats at the hands of the Yankees in World Series play were not the only heartaches Brooklyn fans had to endure during those years. Not by a long shot. On three separate occasions between 1946 and 1951 the club managed to lose the National League pennant on the last day of the season. In 1946 they dropped a best-of-three pennant playoff to the St. Louis Cardinals, and in 1950 they lost the title to the Philadelphia "Whiz Kids" in the last inning of the last game of the season. But the biggest heartache of all came in 1951 when they lost the flag to their hated rivals, the New York Giants, on perhaps the single most famous event in baseball history, Bobby Thomson's two-out, ninth inning, game-winning three-run homer off Ralph Branca in the third and final playoff game. And if losing the pennant wasn't bad enough, the Giants had forced the three-game playoff by overcoming a 16½–game Dodger lead with only a month and a half left in the season.

"You may glory in a team triumphant," wrote Roger Kahn, "but you fall in love with a team in defeat." This was without question true of the Brooklyn Dodgers. In all of baseball there were no more loyal, fanatical and loving fans than the Ebbets Field faithful. The entire borough of Brooklyn lived and died by the fortunes of their beloved

Dodgers. Indeed, it was this loyalty and love for the team that helped in some measure when Jackie Robinson broke the big-league color line in 1947.

Once they saw Robinson's incredible abilities, and once they understood the kind of man he was, Dodger fans simply accepted him as a Dodger. As far as they were concerned, it didn't matter what color any Dodger was, as long as he could help the team achieve that elusive World Championship. If Branch Rickey knew he had the right man in Jackie Robinson, he also knew he had the right city in Brooklyn.

It is a matter of historical record that the Brooklyn Dodgers were the first fully integrated team in baseball history, and a number of elements contributed to the team's success. One was, of course, the great courage and abilities of Jackie Robinson. Another was the way the Dodgers themselves pulled together to fight the ignorance, prejudice and hate they faced because of Jackie's presence on the field. This says quite a bit for the caliber of men who played on those great teams. In the 10 years Robinson played, the Dodgers won five pennants and a World Championship. To win consistently over a decade while playing under the enormous pressure and harsh glare of national media attention was a monumental accomplishment. Robinson's teammates rallied around him, and in doing so set an example for the entire nation in tolerance, understanding and brotherhood.

A third and very important reason for the Dodgers' success was the loyalty and love of the fans. The city of Brooklyn supported their team through the good times and the bad. Yet, for all the support they gave the Dodgers, fans were disappointed year after year as their team either lost the pennant in a tight race or, if they won the title, lost to the Yankees in the World Series. And every year, after another Dodger defeat, the fans kept the spirit alive with their rallying cry of "Wait 'Til Next Year!"

"Next Year" finally came for the Dodgers in 1955 when they beat the hated Yankees in seven games to win their one and only World Championship in Brooklyn. It is well known that Sandy Amoros' running catch of Yogi Berra's slicing line drive down the left-field line in the seventh inning of the seventh game probably saved the Dodgers from yet another defeat. What is not so well known is that Gil Hodges drove in both runs in the Bums' 2–1 victory with a single and a sacrifice fly.

The 1955 Brooklyn Dodgers were an aging team, with all the mainstays on the club well into their thirties. Although no one articulated it, there was a feeling in spring training of that season that if they didn't finally win it all in 1955 they might never get the chance again, and this great club would go down in history without a World Championship to its credit.

"I really felt that 1955 may have been our last chance," recalls Pee Wee Reese. "I was the oldest guy on the club and I had played in six World Series, all against the Yankees, and we had lost every one of them. In 1955 I thought, hell, if we don't win this damn thing this year we may never win it. The fellas didn't sit around and talk about it, but I know we felt it. Funny thing is, we never went into a Series against the Yankees thinking we were underdogs. We always thought we could beat them, but something always happened; it was just one of those things. But we finally did it in 1955."

The Dodgers won the pennant again in 1956, but things returned to normal as the Yankees beat them in seven games, with Don Larsen pitching his historic perfect game in the fifth contest. In 1957 an aging Dodger club finished third, and that winter owner Walter O'Malley moved the franchise to Los Angeles, ending a golden era in baseball history.

During Brooklyn's glory years of the late Forties and early-to-mid-Fifties, the team had many heroes, among them Pete Reiser, Jackie Robinson, Duke Snider, Roy Campanella, Carl Furillo, Billy Cox, Carl Erskine, Clem Laine, Preacher Roe, and Pee Wee Reese; but Gil Hodges was a special favorite of the fans. He was the only player the fanatic but fickle Brooklyn fans didn't boo at one time or another. At Ebbets Field this was nothing short of miraculous. "If I had ever sold or traded Hodges,'' said owner Walter O'Malley, "the Brooklyn fans would hang me, burn me and tear me to pieces."

"Not getting booed at Ebbets Field was an amazing thing," says Clem Labine. "Those fans knew their baseball and Gil was the only player I can remember whom the fans never, I mean never booed. That tells you a lot about the way they felt about him and the kind of man he was."

"He gave everything he was capable of giving all the time," says Carl Erskine, "and I think that the fans knew that when Gil was doing poorly he was still giving his absolute best and that he was hurting worse inside than anybody. If the fans felt bad, they'd have to believe that Gil was feeling even worse. So they showed their respect by just refusing— and this is amazing—just refusing to boo him. I know I heard Joe DiMaggio booed at Yankee Stadium. I heard Stan Musial booed in St. Louis, and I certainly heard a few of my own, but never Gil. This is a very unique thing and I think it speaks volumes for the kind of man Gil was."

As much as the people of Brooklyn loved Gil Hodges, that's how much he loved the city of Brooklyn. In the spring of 1948, at a party given by his landlady, Gil met a pretty young Brooklyn girl from Bay Ridge named Joan Lombardi. He liked Joan at first sight and asked her for a date. The young couple went to see "The Bells of St. Mary's" starring Bing Crosby, and before the year was out, the bells wre ringing for their wedding at St. Gregory's Church in Brooklyn. They bought a home on Bedford Avenue and settled down to raise a family. To the people of Brooklyn Gil Hodges was more than a star player on the city's team; he was a permanent member of the community.

"The city of Brooklyn has always been one of warmth and friendship and Gil loved that," recalls Hodges' friend and attorney Sid Loberfeld. "He wouldn't think of living any-where else. He found a home in Brooklyn."

On off-days or during the off-season Gil could be seen strolling through the neighborhood with his four children or doing some shopping for his wife. He was a devoted family man and the people of Brooklyn looked upon him not only as a sports hero, but as a friend and neighbor too. They admired his strong, quiet demeanor, his gentlemanly ways, his upstanding character and his devotion to family, friends and his religion. More than any other Dodger player, Gil Hodges was Brooklyn's own. And Gil reciprocated by giving his time unselfishly to the community, especially the children. Over the years he appeared at hundreds of benefits and affairs for children and never accepted a fee for his time.

Gil also gave much of his time to the Gil Hodges Little League. "In the mid-Fifties I had the South Highway Little League renamed in Gil's honor," says Sid Loberfeld. "I'll never forget the grand opening. Gil got about six or seven big leaguers to come down. Duke Snider was there, Campy, Roger Craig and others. There were bands and celebrities and politicians. In fact, every year the opening of the little league season was a big event for Gil. But Gil was always giving a lot of his time to the kids and to charities. It was one of his greatest assets.

"Sometimes, after Dodger home games or on off days, Gil would come down to the little league games to watch the kids play. He'd give them pointers and try to help them out. He felt a real responsibility to those kids, and you can bet the kids got a thrill out of it. But that's just the kind of man he was."

As Gil's attorney, Sid Loberfeld was involved with Gil in various business ventures through the years, and in recalling Gil's dealings in this area, Loberfeld says with love and fondness in his voice: "Gil was really no businessman. He was always concerned about the other guy, to make sure the other guy got a square deal. He didn't want to squeeze anybody, so to speak. No, he was no businessman. See, his family was the most important thing in his life, then baseball. Those two things were his whole life."

These sentiments are echoed by many of the men who played for Gil when he managed the Mets. Says former Met shortstop Bud Harrelson, "With Gil you knew that baseball was second; it was not his first love. His first concern was his family, and I think he conveyed that to his players. If you came into the clubhouse, realistically, and said to Gil, 'My wife's really sick and the baby's home,' he'd say, 'Goodbye.' He didn't want you there. He'd rather you go home to your family. And by doing this he was saying something: 'Go, be with your family; that's the most important thing. I'll handle it here. I'll handle the press and everybody.' "

"Gil understood what the important things in life were," says former Met catcher Jerry Grote, "and he tried to teach his players that. To Gil the family was the most important thing. Hell, a ball game was just a ball game. That's not to say Gil didn't think it was important, but he knew that there were more important things to worry about than playing ball. The men who played for him knew this and they respected him for it."

"Anybody that knew Gil loved and respected him," says Sid Loberfeld. "And if you didn't know him personally but you followed him, you came to love him because of the kind of man he was. If baseball had more men like him it would be a great asset to the game. He was genuinely honest, decent and respectful; and he was probably the greatest man of character the game has ever produced."

* * *

IN LOOKING BACK OVER HIS 18–YEAR BIG LEAGUE career, it is clear that Hodges was one of the game's great right-handed power hitters. His first season as a Brooklyn Dodger was 1948, and he struggled throughout, hitting only .249 with 11 home runs and 70 RBIs. But in 1949 he started to come into his own, batting .285 with 23 homers and 115 runs knocked in. From this point Gil's numbers got better and better with each passing season. In 1950 he compiled a .283 average, 32 home runs and 113 RBIs, and followed this with 40 round-trippers and 113 RBIs in 1951. It seemed that nothing could stop Gil. But then, toward the end of the 1952 season and into the World Series, he was seized by his infamous slump that would last through the middle of the 1953 campaign. It was undoubtedly the most trying, frustrating and exasperating period of his big league career.

The Brooklyn Dodgers of Hodges' era were an awesomely powerful offensive machine, but the majority of their power was from the right side of the plate. Campanella, Hodges, Furillo and Robinson were all right-handed swingers. Centerfielder Duke Snider was the only left-handed power threat in the lineup. As a result the Dodgers rarely saw a southpaw on the mound, especially in the cozy confines of Ebbets Field. This was at the heart of Gil's hitting problem. His weakness was the good curveball from a right-hander. When thrown effectively, this pitch appears to be headed directly at the batter's head or body until, at the last second, it breaks over the middle or outside part of the plate. Gil's tendency when thrown the curveball was to "pull out" or "step in the bucket." In other words, instead of striding toward the pitch with his front (left) foot, he stepped toward third base, into "the bucket." It was an involuntary action, and it resulted in his weight and momentum carrying him away from the pitch instead of into it. What's worse, his head came up and his swing was nothing more than a flailing motion. So even when he made contact he wasn't driving the ball and his great size and strength went for naught. Also, by stepping away, Hodges lost the outside part of the plate. Stepping out was something Gil had done since the start of his professional career, but in the early years it had little or no effect on him. He wasn't even aware of this flaw, and just waited for a pitch he could handle. But as the seasons passed his problem became more and more pronounced, and when pitchers became aware of this weakness, Hodges was fed a steady diet of curveballs. Toward the end of the 1952 season and into the World Series, he couldn't buy a hit.

The slump continued well into the start of the 1953 season, and by mid-May the Dodger slugger was hitting a paltry

.187. Duke Snider remembers this period of Gil's career. "I'm sure that underneath Gil agonized beyond anyone's imagination, but he never showed it on the surface. He stayed pretty much on an even keel."

To duck or step away from a baseball that appears to be coming directly at you at over 80 miles per hour is nothing more than an instinctive human response, one hitters must learn to conquer if they want to stay in the big leagues. Some do it easily; others, like Hodges, find it more difficult, and many can never overcome it. Multitudes of minor league hitting phenoms never make it in the big leagues simply because they can't hit a major league curveball. "Lord Charles"—the players' term for the pitch—has ended a good many careers before they began.

Nothing in Gil Hodges's baseball career more vividly illustrates the man's great courage, determination and perseverance than does his fighting this instinct through 18 big league seasons, while compiling an enviable hitting record.

It was Dodger manager Charlie Dressen who finally pinpointed Gil's problem and helped him solve it. During the slump Dressen had team photographer Barney Stein shoot thousands of feet of motion picture film of Gil at the plate. In viewing the film Dressen saw how Gil was striding away from the ball toward third base, and suggested a simple solution to the slugger. He told Gil to keep his front foot where it was, but to move his back foot farther away from the plate. In this manner, when Gil pulled out he would be, in effect, straightening himself out and striding toward the ball.

This simple solution worked, and it probably saved Gil's career. Yet having made this adjustment and having broken out of the slump, there were times when one could see Gil's left leg shaking as he waited for a pitch. When this was pointed out to him, Gil smiled and said, "That's my curveball leg." The fact remains that he spent an entire career facing the toughest right-handed pitching in the National

League, and hit well enough to be among the league leaders in home runs and RBIs every season during his prime from 1949 through 1957.

"Gil was a guess hitter," remembers Duke Snider. "He not only guessed what pitch he was going to be thrown, but the location too. That's pretty tough to do, but being a former catcher he analyzed pitchers exceptionally well. He hit their mistakes. I remember I asked him about it and he said, 'I just know what they're going to try and throw me and where. And if they don't hit the location they're trying for it's not going to surprise me too much. If I'm looking for a curveball low and away and it comes inside, I can adjust to it.' "

Over the course of his 18-year big-league career, Gil Hodges fashioned a record that by now ought to have earned him a plaque in baseball's Hall of Fame. It states in the rules for election that candidates "shall be chosen on the basis of playing ability, integrity, sportsmanship, character, their contribution to the team or teams on which they played and to baseball in general." This being the case, it is a continuing and glaring injustice that Gil Hodges is not enshrined with the greats of the game. As a player and as a man he belongs.

"I feel that someday he'll make the Hall of Fame," says Carl Erskine. "It's really inappropriate to have Reese, Robinson, Campanella and Snider in there and not have Gil. When you take into consideration the setting, the time, the contributions he made, and then you add in the managing which none of the others had, I think he deserves to make it."

"Knowing what a great player he was and what a great guy he was, I think Gil belongs in the Hall of Fame," says Pee Wee Reese. "He belongs and I hope I'm alive to see him get in."

"Gil Hodges is a Hall of Famer," says Duke Snider. "In my estimation the wrong people are voting, people who didn't know him very well or what he meant to the team. Gil was a team player. There wasn't a selfish bone in his body. We were all cogs in a wheel, and that wheel was dominant in the late Forties and Fifties.

"They draw a fine line between who gets into the Hall of Fame and who doesn't, but the people who are drawing that line really shouldn't be. I've talked to some of these writers who say that some guy will get into the Hall, but not on the first ballot. That's ridiculous. Either somebody is a Hall of Famer or he isn't. If he's going to get in on the third or fourth ballot, then why not the first? It doesn't make any sense. I'm sure Gil's going to get in. He deserves it. It's just a shame that his family and firends have to wait so long for that day."

"It's just one of those things," observes Sid Loberfeld. "For one thing, if Gil was around he'd never want to push. That just wasn't his way. Also keep in mind that many of the writers who saw him play aren't around anymore. There's no question he was one of the greatest fielding first basemen the game has ever known, and as a slugger he was right up there with the best. He was a team player and a team leader who was greatly respected by the players, the fans and everybody in the game. And then you have to take into consideration what he did as a manager with the 1969 New York Mets. But perhaps more important than any of this was the example he set, especially for the kids. He was a real gentleman and a man of character. They just don't make them like him anymore."

* * *

WHEN THE DODGERS PULLED UP STAKES IN BROOKLYN and headed for Los Angeles in 1957, Gil, like everybody in Brooklyn, was saddened by the move. "I just don't want to move," said Gil at the time. "I live in Brooklyn. I'm not just a Dodger ballplayer. Brooklyn is my home."

Indeed, a great and memorable era in baseball history had come to an end. For the first time since its establishment in 1876, the National League did not have a franchise in New York. Yet while the Dodgers were in Brooklyn, they left their mark not only on baseball history but on American social history as well. Few teams have been more popular or loved by all of America than were the Dodgers. Their legacy as the battling underdogs, as everyman's team, who, after so many heartbreaking setbacks and so many years of trying, finally won it all in 1955, is as much a part of American folklore as it is of baseball history.

And it was in Brooklyn, with the Dodgers, that a black man played in the major leagues for the first time. It changed forever the course of baseball history, and more importantly, the course of American history. Its effects were felt throughout every strata of American society. It is ironic yet in many ways fitting that one of the first and most important steps taken in 20th century America for equality and justice, and against the poisons of racism, prejudice and segregation, was not taken in the White House or in the hallowed halls of Congress, but on a ball field in Brooklyn by a great and courageous American named Jackie Robinson. The triumph of Robinson and his Dodger teammates was a victory for us all.

Looking back with hindsight, the members of that great Dodger team can now see the impact they had on a nation, but at the time they were unaware of it. "It amazes all of us how popular that team was and how it's remained that way through the years," says Carl Erskine. "At the time we didn't think we were affecting anybody's life. We just went out there and tried to win ball games. We were just trying to do our jobs. It was hard for us who were close to it to understand the effect we were having. But looking back at it now it's easy to see why that team was so unique."

"It was the right time in history," reflects Preacher Roe. "With Jackie breaking the color line and then other black players coming into the major leagues, it was an historic time in baseball and I guess in America. Plus, we had a great team; we had a lot of success. And you have to give the people of Brooklyn a lot of credit, too. They loved and supported that team so much. They were really like the tenth man on the field."

"We were part of history being made, but we really didn't realize it at the time," says Clem Labine. "There was Jackie, of course, and all the other men on that team. It was definitely a unique and colorful collection of personalities. And that club had a lot of character; it had to when you consider the pressure we were put under and we still won pennants. But at the time we were just going out there trying to win ballgames and not really realizing the kind of impact we were having."

"Starting in 1947, when Jackie came up, we knew we had something special with that club," says Duke Snider, "but I don't think any of us realized back then how popular that team would become. You know, we really were America's team. It just amazes me how the legend and history of that team is passed on from one generation to the next. I go to these baseball-card conventions sometimes, and young people come up to me and talk in detail about things that happened with the Brooklyn Dodgers years before they were born, things that I can't even recall. It's really a phenomenal thing the way it has been carried on. I'm just happy that I was a part of it."

"A lot of the magic of the Brooklyn Dodgers had to do with Jackie Robinson," says Pee Wee Reese, "but also the city of Brooklyn. In those days Brooklyn was looked at as kind of a joke. I remember when I was in the service and we'd see a movie and somebody in the film mentioned Brooklyn, it always got a laugh. But Brooklyn was a great place. It had its own unique personality. It's funny, people would talk like you were going to a foreign country when you went to Brooklyn. But it was a great place to be, and those were wonderful years we spent there. We made a little history, didn't we?"

When the Dodgers moved to the West Coast, Gil Hodges had his reservations about leaving his Brooklyn home. But there was one bright spot for Gil, or so he thought at the time—the dimensions of the ball park where the Dodgers would play in 1958. Until Dodger Stadium in Chavez Ravine was completed, the team's home would be the Los Angeles Coliseum. Built primarily for football and track, the Coliseum is huge, holding upwards of 90,000 people, but wholly unsuited for baseball. To Gil's delight, however, the left field foul pole was only 250 feet from home plate. He figured on having his best home run season ever in 1958. He didn't, and, in fact, had the worst year of his career since his rookie season of 1948. Adjusting his swing to pull everything toward the short left field porch, Gil hit only .259 with 24 homers and 64 RBIs. In 1959 he bounced back and was a major factor in the Dodgers' drive to the World Championship, batting .276 with 25 home runs and 88 runs knocked in. But 1959 was to be his last season as an everyday player.

In Gil's last two years as a Dodger, playing mostly as a part-timer and pinch hitter, he batted only .198 with 8 homers in 1960, and .242 with 8 home runs in 1961. By the end of the '61 season Hodges and Duke Snider were the only players left from the great Brooklyn Dodger dynasty of the Fifties, and it was time for the club to rebuild.

hool photo of Gil (*left*) and his older brother Bob, taken in 1930, just prior to the
odges family's moving to Petersburg, Indiana.

, second from right in bottom row, as a junior high school basketball player in
6.

Pike County, Indiana, basketball champions of 1941, Petersburg High, led b "Bud" Hodges, number 11, and Bob Hodges, number 7.

The St. Joseph's College baseball team in the spring of 1942. Gil is in the midd row, fourth from the right.

as a young Brooklyn Dodger during spring training in 1950.

A brilliant defensive first baseman, Gil makes a fine grab of a foul pop-up in 195[action at the Polo Grounds.

Gil knocks in teammates Jackie Robinson (*left*) and Pee Wee Reese (*right*) with a inside-the-park homer in 1954.

ove: The great Jackie
binson, Gil's teammate
ten seasons.

Dodger captain, Hall
Famer Pee Wee Reese.

Gil bats against the Chicago White Sox at the Los Angeles Coliseum in the 1959 World Series, his last as a Dodger.

PART THREE

The Skipper

THREE

Oh my God, we're World Champions!

In the winter of 1961 the newly formed New York Mets of the National League were being assembled through the expansion draft and player purchases. The Mets purchased Hodges from the Dodgers, bringing him home to finish out his playing career in the place where he belonged, New York. The Mets' front office also knew that Gil, being one of the most beloved players in the City's history, would draw fans to the ball park.

Gil Hodges was 38 when he joined the Mets, far past his prime and in need of surgery on an injured right knee. The Mets' home park was to be the Polo Grounds until a new stadium could be built. One can only imagine how strange it must have felt for Gil to be playing home games in the park of the Dodgers' arch rivals, the New York Giants, while wearing a new uniform that was a combination of Dodger blue, Giant orange and Yankee pinstripes.

Because of his ailing right knee, Gil played in only 54 games for the original Mets, but in the first game of their history he hit the club's first home run, a solo blast in the fourth inning of an 11–4 loss to St. Louis.

Gil's knee was operated on in 1963, and after playing in only 11 games for the Mets, he retired as an active player to take over as skipper of the lowly Washington Senators. This was a move that surprised many who knew him. It seemed that Gil's quiet, introspective personality was ill suited to the high-pressure life of a big-league manager. "It was a surprise to me that Gil became a manager," says Carl Erskine. "I think most of us felt that it wasn't that Gil didn't know the game. From that standpoint no one was surprised that he became successful. It was handling players; that's where we had our doubts. I mean, here's Durocher, here's Dressen, the old firebrand-type managers. No one could picture Gil holding a clubhouse meeting and chewing somebody out. But we watched him and we saw that he could be very firm, but always fair. Then of course he won the World Series in 1969, and we all saw that silent strength come through."

"It was a surprise to me," says Carl Furillo. "I knew Gil as well as anybody on the club, and I didn't think he had the right kind of personality to become a manager. Once he took the job though, I knew he'd be successful."

One person who was not surprised by Gil becoming a big league skipper was Sid Loberfeld. "Being a manager of a big-league team is a challenge that almost nobody rejects," says Loberfeld. "Gil was always a team leader and the other Dodgers looked up to him. He had all the qualities to be a great leader, and he was."

From the day Hodges took control of the Senators they began to improve steadily. Finishing last in 1963, they moved up to eighth in '64 and '65, seventh in '66, and in 1967 they reached sixth place.

"I had a chance to see Hodges in action as a manager before I played for him in New York," remembers former Met third baseman Ed Charles, who played for the Kansas City A's during the years Gil managed Washington. "I saw how he shaped a bunch of ragamuffins over there in Washington. Before Gil took over, that club had a defeated attitude. They felt like they were going to lose every game, and the other teams knew it. Hell, we just threw our gloves on the field and those guys were beat.

"But then Hodges took over, and I'll tell you, things just turned around. They were a different team. He shaped their attitude. Now those same guys are putting out 120 percent every game. So now we go into Washington and it's hell trying to beat those guys. They fight us every inch of the way. See, motivation is a big part of managing, probably what managing is all about, and Gil Hodges had to be one of the all-time greats as far as motivating guys and getting them to put out."

Frank Howard, who played with Hodges for four years in Los Angeles, played for him when Gil managed the Senators. "Let's face it," says Howard, "we didn't have the talent on the Senators to compete with the powerhouse clubs in the American League at that time. But Gil ran a super ball game. He instilled pride in his players; he motivated them. He was a great believer in basic fundamentals. Gil really stressed that. He used to say, 'Hey, we may not match up talent-wise, but the one thing we can do is be fundamentally sound; throw to the right base, hustle all the time, hit the cut-off man, run the bases smartly, do what you're supposed to do and we'll be in the ball game.' Gil stressed this and we worked on fundamentals constantly. The result was we moved up four places in the standings in as many years."

During the time Hodges was with Washington, the New York Mets organization was building from within, signing talented young players and slowly bringing them along in the system. As players like Tom Seaver, Bud Harrelson, Jerry Koosman and Cleon Jones became ready for the big leagues, the Mets wanted to bring in a manager to shape and mold these young players into winners. So in the fall of 1967 they traded pitcher Bill Denehy and cash to the Washington Senators for the right to sign Gil Hodges to a managerial contract. It was a turning point in the franchise's history.

The New York club Gil inherited was one full of young, raw talent, especially in the pitching department. It was the kind of talent that, given the right handling and direction, could turn the fortunes of the franchise around. The first two things Gil did upon assuming command was to firmly establish himself as undisputed boss, and to carefully evaluate the players he had to work with.

"Before Hodges came over there was really no discipline," says Jerry Grote. "Wes Westrum was the manager and he was always second-guessing everybody so we didn't have a whole lot of respect for him. In 1968 Gil came in and established the fact that, hey, I'm the boss and you don't cross me. He established a real tough line just by the force of his personality. It was just what the club needed. Also, Gil didn't say much that first year; he just kind of sat back and watched. He wanted to see what kind of talent he had to work with."

Gil managed the Mets to 73 wins in 1968, by far their best season ever. It was evident to anyone who watched the club that season that they had improved by leaps and bounds under Gil's steady leadership. His most important accomplishment that year, however, was not the fact that the Mets won more games—although that was important—but that he had instilled pride, self-confidence and a winning attitude in his young players, an attitude unknown on any previous Mets team.

But Gil was unable to finish out the '68 season on the Mets' bench. In the late summer of that year the pressures and stress of six campaigns as a big league skipper, coupled with Gil's heavy smoking, finally took their toll.

On September 24, 1968, the Mets were in Atlanta for a night game against the Braves. In the second inning of the game Gil got up from the bench, and asking trainer Gus Mauch to accompany him, went to lie down in the clubhouse. He had pains in his chest and was shivering with chills. Mauch saw that the manager's color was ashen white. The trainer immediately called the Atlanta team doctor, Harry Rogers, into the clubhouse to examine Gil. Rogers made tests of Gil's heart, chest and blood pressure, and felt that he could wait until morning before checking into a hospital for a more extensive examination.

Hodges lay on a training table for about an hour but didn't feel any better; in fact, he felt worse. Trainer Mauch didn't want to take any chances, and insisted that Gil check into a hospital immediately. The two men took a cab to Atlanta's Crawford W. Long Hospital, where an examination revealed that he had suffered a myocardial infarct, a mild heart attack. At 44 years old, Gil Hodges was lucky to be alive.

For a week prior to his attack, Gil had felt pains in his chest but told no one. He continued hitting infield practice and fungoes, and pitching batting practice. "Gil had had a bad cold for a week or so, " remembers former Met pitching coach Rube Walker. "He hadn't been feeling right, but he never complained. I didn't even realize he wasn't feeling well until he left the dugout and asked Mauch to go with him into the clubhouse."

The night of the heart attack Gil had pitched 15 minutes of batting practice in Atlanta's humid late-summer heat. "He bent over when he was finished," recalls coach Joe Pignatano, "and I couldn't tell if he was trying to catch his breath or if his knee was bothering him."

"Did I know what it was?" mused Hodges later. "I suppose so. Yes. Did I *want* to know what it was? No."

After examining Hodges, Doctor Lincoln Bishop told the press: "I would describe his condition as good. He is breathing well, is quite comfortable and doesn't seem to be in any pain. I would not have any doubts that after a proper period of rest, he would be able to return to his full-time duties."

Gil recuperated in the Atlanta hospital for almost a month. His wife Joan had flown down the night he was taken ill and stayed by her husband's side throughout his recovery period. Thousands of get-well cards, letters and phone calls poured in. As always, everybody was pulling for Gil. For the first 10 days after his attack, the doctors would not permit him to watch or listen to any sporting event, fearing the excitement might aggravate his condition. But then they relented and let him watch the Tiger-Cardinal World Series on TV. "The doctor wasn't so anxious to let me watch the World Series," said Gil. "He thought I would get excited. But I convinced him that a game between St. Louis and

Detroit wouldn't excite me. The only thing that excites me is a New York Mets game."

That winter serious questions were raised as to whether or not Gil would be able to continue managing. But he never really gave retirement a thought. "The only scare moment I had," he said after his release from the hospital, "was when they told me it was a slight heart attack.

"The doctors have told me you treat the convalescence from a mild heart attack the same as a serious one," he continued. "I have to get down to 200 pounds, do things slowly, build up to normal activity, everything in moderation. Besides taking it easy, the only other thing I have to do is give up smoking. The doctors say if I do this I'll be as good as new." Then, showing his dry sense of humor, Gil added, "I know I've been laid up a long time; my wife is beating me at gin."

*   *   *

WHEN GIL RETURNED TO HIS MANAGERIAL DUTIES IN the spring of 1969, he made an optimistic prediction about how his young team would do in the upcoming season. "I would hope," said Hodges, "that we would win 85 games." The talent to do so was there. The Mets had an incredibly strong young pitching staff. Still, the thought of the heretofore lowly Mets winning upwards of 80 games was hard for many people to accept.

After the team's promising showing in 1968, the mood on the Mets was a positive one. People were talking about the club becoming a solid contender in two or three years, and everybody expected them to continue to improve in 1969. Nobody, however, expected them to do what they did.

In one of the most exciting and memorable seasons in baseball history, the 1969 New York Mets brought all of America to its feet cheering with their drive to the World Championship. Their timing couldn't have been better. As the most violent and turbulent decade in modern American history came to an end—an era that shook the nation to its very foundations and left deep scars across the face of the country—the Mets brought people together as nothing else could. As underdogs, the Mets appealed to a basic instinct in all Americans. In fact, they were the most *under* underdog in the history of our National Game. As 100–to–1 shots to go all the way, their heroics on the ball field overshadowed even man's first walk on the moon. Neil Armstrong's lunar stroll may have been a "giant leap for mankind," but the Mets' victory was a triumph for the common man, the very heart and soul of America. Never before in the annals of sports history did a team lift the spirit of the nation as did the Mets in 1969. That year, from Boston to Los Angeles, from Bangor to Seattle, from Detroit to Baton Rouge, America was a Mets fan.

Up until the 1969 season the Mets were looked upon as the clown princes of baseball. Sure they were lovable, but they lost year after year. As such, their rise to the 1969 World Championship was one of the most dramatic sagas in the history of American sport.

And behind all the excitement and drama stood one man, Gil Hodges. He had molded the team and had gotten the best from each man; he had steadied them and made them believe in themselves, and he led them to what is perhaps the most inspiring and exciting World Championship in baseball history.

The 1969 season stands as a tribute to Gil Hodges' ability as a leader, and to his managerial genius. Gil himself described managing as "mostly common sense," and certainly that is part of it. But managing is also the ability to motivate men, to keep 25 different personalities content, and to get the most from each player. Hodges did this as few managers have been able to do. The 1969 Mets were not the most talented team in baseball, but Hodges used the entire squad, maximizing each man's strengths and minimizing his weaknesses. He platooned in four of the eight starting positions, and under this system every member of the team made a major contribution to their success.

And throughout it all, while America fell in love with and went wild over the Mets, Gil remained calm and reserved, sitting in the dugout watching, planning, and always staying two steps ahead of the opposition.

"We had 25 players and we had 25 heroes in the final six weeks of the '69 season," says Tom Seaver. "And the biggest hero of all was Gil Hodges. When everyone else got excited, when we were scrambling to catch the Cubs, Gil remained calm. The tenser the situation, the more he concentrated. He never wavered, never came within a mile of panic, always observing, always maneuvering, always thinking.

"We were managed by an infallible genius in the final six weeks of that season," continues Seaver. "Every move Gil made worked. If he lifted a starter, the relief pitcher was brilliant; if he decided to stick with a starter who seemed to be tiring, the man revived. If he let a weak hitter bat in a critical situation, the man came through with a hit; if he called on a pinch hitter, the man delivered. Gil seemed to have absolute faith in his own judgment, his own methods, and we came to share it. He could do no wrong. If he had decided to have me pinch-hit for Cleon Jones, I would have hit a home run. No doubt about it."

"Gil was always in complete control of himself," says Ed Charles. "No matter what the situation he just never wavered. He steadied the ball club."

"All I know is that I saw Gil smiling more that year than I'd ever seen him smiling in my life," recalls former Met first baseman Donn Clendenon.

Gil's rule for handling his men was a simple one: "Be it to the number 25 man on your club, just as much as to the number one man." But Gil knew, too, that a ball club is made up of 25 different and unique individuals. "Gilly treated everybody alike, but handled each man differently," says coach Joe Pignatano. "He was a master at it."

"He knew that everybody could not be handled alike, " adds Donn Clendenon. "He knew that there had to be differences between how you handled each man, but he would not make it a glaring difference to show partiality."

"Gil was warmer in 1969 than he'd been in 1968," says Tom Seaver. "He smiled more often and joked more often. I began to realize that he'd spent his first year studying his players, assessing their skills and measuring their personalities.

"Gil set rules, and his rules applied equally to every man on the club. You made the bus on time; you got to the field on time. He played no favorites. If he thought you'd done something wrong, if you hadn't hustled, if you hadn't concentrated, he let you knew. He didn't scream, and he didn't yell, but he got his message across."

As a strategist and tactician, Hodges was nearly flawless in 1969. It seemed that every move he made was the right one. He knew his team and what each man was capable of in a given situation. "We knew that whatever Gil did was going to be right," says Jerry Grote. "He did not make mistakes. We might not produce or deliver, but he always made the right move. He never cost us a ball game. Never. In all the years I played, for all the different managers, he's the only one I can say that about."

"I can say this, and I can say it with all honesty," says former Mets left fielder Cleon Jones; "if it wasn't for Gil Hodges we would not have won. If we had been managed by anybody else we wouldn't have won. Gill was the difference. He instilled confidence in us and made us believe we could win."

It would be naive to think that every player on the club fully agreed with Gil's system and managerial philosophy. "Sure, some guys would say that Gil wasn't fair," says Jerry Grote, "but those would be the guys that were always in trouble with him, and they're not being fair to Gil."

From the beginning outfielder Ron Swoboda and first baseman Ed Kranepool were vehemently opposed to being platooned. Both had been darlings of Met fans during the losing years when they were hungry for young heroes, and both had been used to playing every day. All this changed when Hodges arrived and the two became part of his platoon system. They resented this and publicly criticized Hodges.

"Swoboda and Kranepool were the only ones ever to argue with Gil," remembers a teammate, "but they were both spoiled kids at the time, and Gil had his problems with them."

Still, Hodges put personality problems aside and, using Swoboda and Kranepool as he saw fit, each player made big contributions to the success of the '69 Mets. They may not have agreed with Gil, but they respected him. "We were set in our ways," says Ed Kranepool, "and they were not the right ways. It was a bad club and I was rotten. He made me a better player and a better person."

* * *

LIKE BABE RUTH'S CALLED HOME RUN, JOE DIMAGgio's 56-game hitting streak, Jackie Robinson's breaking of the color line, Bobby Thomson's "shot heard 'round the world," and Don Larsen's perfect World Series game, the saga of the 1969 Mets transcends the boundaries of baseball history and holds a special place in American folklore.

The historical setting of the "Miracle of '69," as it's come to be known, was the major factor in the team's unprecedented national popularity. The country was reeling from the violence and social upheaval of the Sixties. The Mets were just the tonic America needed to help take its mind off the troubles and heartaches of the ending decade. The nation embraced them. What's more, in their own way the Mets reaffirmed a basic American principle: That with enough effort, perseverance, hard work, and a little bit of luck, the little man, the common man, the underdog, could fight his way to the top.

The key to the Mets' success was their strong young pitching staff. Their starting rotation consisted of Tom Seaver, Jerry Koosman and Gary Gentry, with Nolan Ryan, veteran Don Cardwell and Jim McAndrew sharing the fourth and occasional fifth spot. The bullpen was also strong with veteran righthanders Ron Taylor, Cal Koonce and lefty screwballer Tug McGraw. It was Hodges' idea to make McGraw into a stopper after many failed attempts by the organization to use the young southpaw as a starter. One day, early in the '69 season, Gil called McGraw into his office and told the lefty he would be moved to the bullpen. "Gil said to me, 'I'm telling you this because I believe this ball club is ready, and we need a good reliever, a stopper,'" recalls Tug of his meeting with Hodges. "To me, that was like 'Holy Cow!' This is for real. We're not fooling around here, and if I want to be part of it, this is what I have to do."

"I could see the strength of our pitching staff in spring training," remembers Ed Charles. "You watch guys like Seaver, Koosman, Gentry, McGraw and Ryan throwing a baseball, and you know you're going to win some games."

"What a lot of people don't realize is how brilliant Hodges and [pitching coach] Rube Walker were in handling the pitchers," says Jerry Grote. "They had a system. First off, in spring training Rube used to walk around with a counter in his hand. After a certain number of throws per day a pitcher was through. That was it. It didn't matter if the throws were warm-ups, batting practice, throws from the outfield, anything. After a certain amount that was it.

"Also, Gil and Rube stressed the right mechanics. They turned those young guys into pitchers, not just throwers. They taught them to use their bodies and legs to pitch and not just their arms. Look at the results. Guys like Seaver, Koosman, Ryan and McGraw each pitched over 20 years in the big leagues. That's an amazing thing, especially when you consider that all of them were hard throwers, and usually hard throwers burn out their arms a lot quicker than junkball pitchers. Not many people give him credit for it, but Gil really knew pitching. Look at the coaching staff. They were mostly catchers, and catchers know pitchers better than anybody. Gil started as a catcher, Rube Walker was a catcher, Joe Pignatano was a catcher and so was Yogi. The only guy who wasn't was Eddie Yost. Gil and Rube knew pitching and how to take care of and develop young arms so they last."

"One thing you have to know about Gil is how thoroughly he studied every aspect of the game," reflects Duke Snider.

"He and Rube were great friends and would spend hours and hours talking baseball. The both of them really studied and analyzed pitchers. It doesn't surprise me that they had so much success with that pitching staff. I would give Gil a lot more credit for that than most people would."

"One of the great things about that staff is we all helped each other," says Jerry Koosman. "We would watch each other pitch and if one of us was doing something wrong we'd find out about it right away. But that was one of the great things about the team; we all helped each other when we could. We were all always rooting for each other. It was a great group of guys."

The biggest strength of the club's everyday lineup was its defense. The 1969 Mets were a team built on pitching and defense, with an adequate offense considering the strength of the pitching staff. Behind the plate was the best defensive catcher of his era and a master handler of pitchers, Jerry Grote. Said Johnny Bench of Grote, "If Grote and I were on the same team, I'd have to play third base."

"Let me tell you something about Jerry Grote," says Ed Charles; "He was a winner. Jerry was one of those guys from the old school. He was a hard-nosed, no-nonsense type of guy. He really took control out there. The pitchers were comfortable with him and he knew those pitchers as well as Gil or Rube or anybody. Maybe he didn't hit .300, but he was a helluva clutch hitter. I don't know how you can measure how valuable Jerry was to us, the way he handled the pitchers, the way he took charge, his toughness, his attitude, his defense. The man was a winner."

At first base the club started the season with Ed Kranepool, while Ken Boswell and Al Weis shared duties at second. The shortstop was the team spark plug, Bud Harrelson. "Of all the guys on our club, Buddy Harrelson was the nucleus," says Jerry Koosman. "The guy went out there every day and took control of the infield. He ran the outfield. He knew all us pitchers and how to play every hitter. He just made us all look like all-stars." Tom Seaver, Bud Harrelson's friend and roommate, summed it up best when he said, "The Mets cannot win without Bud Harrelson at shortstop."

At third base for the '69 Mets were veteran Ed Charles and youngster Wayne Garrett, and in the outfield the club had Cleon Jones in left, Tommie Agee in center, with Ron Swoboda and Art Shamsky sharing the right-field job. Right field was the only weak spot on defense; so Hodges replaced either Swoboda or Shamsky with rookie Rod Gaspar in the late innings of games in which the Mets held a lead.

The only element missing from the Mets lineup was a power hitter who could turn a game around with one swing. This void was filled by general manager Johnny Murphy when he acquired veteran slugger Donn Clendenon from the Montreal Expos just before the midnight trading deadline on June 15. Clendenon not only provided the power the Mets needed, but he also became a team leader.

"Donn added a lot of polish to our ball club," says Bud Harrelson. "We had a lot of raw talent, but a lot of inexperience too. When Clink came over he added class and confidence. He came to hit home runs and he was hitting them; I'm talking awesome tape measure shots. We were in awe of him. He was like a big brother. I mean, this guy could do it."

"When we obtained Donn Clendenon from the Montreal Expos, I knew he'd help us," says Tom Seaver. "We needed someone who could hit the ball out of the park, someone with Donn's proven power."

"When I came to the Mets I had a long talk with Gil and I knew what he wanted from me," recalls Clendenon. "He wanted me to take charge a little and to help build confidence in the young players. This was a new role for me. I was never a rah-rah, talk-it-up kind of guy, but with the Mets it was different. I used to joke and clown around a lot. If I saw a young player with his head down I'd go and talk to him. You see, it's an amazing thing with young minds. If you can build confidence, if you can make a young player truly believe he's the best, it's absolutely amazing what he can do.

That's what I tried to do in my way. It was a wonderful thing to see those youngsters gain the confidence they needed. They thought they were unbeatable, and because of that they were.

"When I first arrived in New York everybody was talking about next year," continues Clendenon, "how they were going to win it next year. I said, 'What about this year? We can win it this year. You want to know why? Because the Cubs are looking over their shoulder at us. You know that you can't win a race if you're looking over your shoulder at the guy behind you. We can win it this year!' "

For as much as Clendenon contributed to the Mets, the young team also gave his sagging career a boost. "There's no question that Clendenon added a lot to our team," says pitcher Gary Gentry, "but we helped him out too. He was in Montreal on a last place expansion club going nowhere. Then he comes to a young team that has a shot at winning it and it really revived him. It really gave him a purpose."

Another leader on the club was 35-year-old third baseman Ed Charles. As the oldest member of the team he was nicknamed "Pops," but Pops, also known as "The Glider" for his smooth style, could still show the youngsters a thing or two about the game. "As senior member of the club, I knew the role Gil wanted me to play," says Charles. "He wanted me to be a stabilizing influence on the younger players, and I accepted that role. When a young guy is having problems it's easy for him to get down, so you have to be able to talk to him and say the right things. They can't always go to the manager; they need one of their own to talk to, and that was the role I played. Plus, leading by example on the field by always giving 110 percent."

"The Glider was an older man, but he was hungry," says Bud Harrelson. "And if he, at his age, could hustle and move, it certainly should be easier for us younger guys. We learned from him. If he could try so hard and hustle, then why not us?"

A member of the '69 Mets whose contributions are often overlooked was veteran righthander Don Cardwell. He had only an 8–10 record that year, but he won some big ball games, and beyond that, had a strong influence on the young pitching staff. "Don Cardwell was the individual on that staff that really helped mold those young pitchers," recalls Jerry Grote. "He was a man they all looked up to. I remember him sitting with the young pitchers, a Cutty Sark in his hand, and they'd all talk about pitching and ways to get guys out, and when Cardwell spoke they listened."

"Cardwell led by example," says Gary Gentry. "Cardy went out there and worked his butt off. He was a lot like Gil; he was quiet, but he could just look at you and make you know you did something wrong."

"I think Gil wanted me to take a leadership role with the younger pitchers," says Cardwell. "It was really no big deal. If I'd seen one of them pitch and I thought they did something wrong I'd tell them. Or maybe I'd point out a certain area where I thought they could improve. We're talking about some pretty incredible young arms, and I just tried to help when I could to make them better pitchers."

Another major factor in the Mets' success was the camaraderie on the club. The members of the team got along very well with each other. On some championship clubs this element is not important; on the 1969 Mets it was one of the keys to their rise.

"I think that was one of the most important factors," says Cleon Jones. "We were a team that got along with each other. It was a great group of guys and we held a real fondness for our teammates. Different guys would get together and go out; families would get together for cookouts. It really was a unique and wonderful thing. This helped because we were always rooting for each other to do well. Everybody stood up for each other. If somebody threw at one of us at the plate, our pitchers would retaliate. Koosman wouldn't hesitate to throw at somebody. Seaver took a little time to come around. I remember we were playing the Cardinals and Bob Gibson threw at somebody, so Seaver let one of the Cardinals have it. I always had respect for Seaver, but I gained even more respect for him that day because I saw what kind of man he was. What he was saying to Gibson was, 'Hey, you do that again and I'll knock your ass off. It doesn't matter what you do to me, because you have to come up and I'll do the same to you!' That attitude really helped us. Hell, we had the hardest throwing staff in baseball; who the hell wants to get hit by a pitch from Seaver or Koosman or Ryan or any of our guys?

"See, we really were a team that looked out for each others. I'm sure it all goes back to Gil Hodges and the way he molded us together. Everybody had a specific role, and you knew exactly what your job was. Some players didn't always agree with Gil, but you can't argue with the results."

"It was a very close-knit team," says Don Cardwell. "Everybody just blended together."

"You could just see everybody meshing together as players and as personalities," says Jerry Grote. "It was a team effort in everything we did. It was a perfect blend of older guys and younger ones, all molded by Gil into a tight unit. It was such a cross-section on that team: Garrett from Florida, a few guys from California, me from Texas, Koos from Minnesota, Kranepool from New York, Glider from the Midwest, guys from all over the country, all different personalities, and all molded together by Gil."

*　*　*

FOR A YOUNG BALL CLUB TO WIN IT MUST HAVE confidence in itself; a feeling that they are a match for any team and can handle any situation that arises in a ball game. As manager, Gil Hodges worked hard to instill this confidence in his young players. The 1969 Mets' confidence started to build in spring training. "I remember we were all sitting around talking one day in training camp," says Jerry

Grote, "me, Seaver, Koosman and a couple of other guys, and we started to analyze the other teams in the division. We realized they weren't that strong, except for maybe the Cubs, and that we could definitely finish second, and maybe had a shot at first. Nobody said anything to the writers, but we all felt that we had a shot."

"During training camp in the spring of 1969, Bud Harrelson, Jerry Grote, Nolan Ryan and I often went fishing at night." Tom Seaver recalls. "While we fished, we talked about almost everything, including baseball. 'You know,' one of us said early in training camp, 'we could win our division if we play up to our potential.' The other three of us didn't disagree. We didn't talk that way too loudly, because we knew if the sportswriters heard us, they'd scoff, and if the average baseball fan heard us, he'd laugh, and if the oddsmakers in Las Vegas heard us, they'd ignore us. But the four of us—Harrelson, Grote, Ryan and me—and just about everybody else on our ball club didn't really care what the oddsmakers said, didn't care if the sportswriters scoffed and the fans laughed. We wanted to win. We felt we could win."

The Mets started the season in their usual fashion by losing to the expansion Montreal Expos 11–10 in the season opener. But by May 21 the Mets had an 18–18 record. It was the latest point in any season in the club's history that they had reached the .500 plateau. "The press made a big deal of it when we reached .500," says Jerry Grote. "There were headlines in the paper and all. But we knew we were better than that. I remember Tom Seaver saying, 'This is only the beginning. We're going to go a lot farther than this.' "

For a time it didn't look like the young Mets were going anywhere, despite Seaver's promise. After reaching the .500 mark the club proceeded to lose five games in a row. This slide put them at 18–23, in fifth place, nine games behind the front-running Cubs.

Then the magic began to happen.

On May 28 the Mets beat the San Diego Padres 1–0 in 11 innings. It was the beginning of the longest winning streak in club history. On June 3 they won their sixth in a row to put their record at 24–23. But it didn't stop there. They kept on winning and on June 3 defeated the Giants 9–4 for their eleventh straight victory. The streak put them in second place, seven games behind Chicago.

"I swear, it was electricity going through the team," recalls Tom Seaver. "Everybody felt the same charge. We began getting stronger and stronger and feeling more and more confident. It went on from there, building."

The real test came in early July when the first place Cubs came to New York for a three-game series. The Mets were 45–34, only five games behind Chicago, and the series loomed as the most important in the club's history. The Cubs were a formidable opponent. Managed by Leo Durocher, they had a powerhouse lineup including Ernie Banks, Ron Santo, Billy Williams, ex-Met Jim Hickman and Randy Hundley. They had a strong keystone combination with Glenn Beckert at second and Don Kessinger at short, and a solid pitching staff led by Ferguson Jenkins, Ken Holtzman and Bill Hands.

This "David and Goliath" showdown between the Mets and the Cubs attracted the attention of the nation. "The eyes of the nation will stray from moon countdowns and tax reform to a puzzling phenomenon," observed the New York Times, "the sudden rise of the New York Mets from baseball urchins to heroes. People will be wondering how a team that lost 737 games in seven seasons could now be challenging for the top."

Most experts felt the young Mets didn't stand a chance in the series and would be a bundle of nerves, while the veteran Cubs would be composed and ready for the challenge. In reality, the opposite was true. "Everybody thought we were going to be nervous," recalls Bud Harrelson, "but we weren't. We had nothing to lose. We weren't supposed to be there in the first place."

"The pressure really wasn't on us to the degree it was on the Cubs," says Ed Charles. "We were a young club and nobody had picked us to win anything. Hell, we had nothing to lose. Now the Cubbies, they were the veteran team. They were supposed to win the division. The pressure was really on them more than us."

"I remember I went over to the Cub clubhouse to see Banks and Ferguson and some of the other guys, and man, there was tension in there," says Donn Clendenon. "And these guys were seasoned veterans. Then you went over into our clubhouse and the guys were laughing, playing cards and kidding around. There was a big difference."

"We really didn't feel any pressure," remembers Jerry Grote. "We didn't have anything to prove and we didn't have anything to lose. We were doing better than anybody expected. But we also felt confident we could win."

"Nobody feels any pressure here," said second baseman Ken Boswell before the series started. "We're all too young. It's like fighting for the high school championship."

In the first game of the series the Mets were losing 3–1 in the bottom of the ninth. They had gotten only one hit through eight innings off Cub starter Ferguson Jenkins. Ken Boswell led off the ninth pinch-hitting for Jerry Koosman and lifted a fly ball toward Cub rookie center fielder Don Young. Young lost the ball in the background of the crowd and it dropped at his feet. Boswell slid safely into second. After Tommie Agee fouled out to Ernie Banks, Donn Clendenon came up and lined a shot to left-center. Young ran over and made a brilliant play, grabbing the ball in the webbing of his glove. Then he crashed into the wall and the ball sprang loose. Clendenon slid into second and Boswell into third. The next man up, Cleon Jones, ripped a double into left scoring Boswell and Clendenon and the game was tied at three. Art Shamsky was then intentionally walked, and Wayne Garrett grounded out to second, moving the runners up. With two out and two on Ed Kranepool faced Ferguson Jenkins. Jenkins fooled Kranepool on a low, outside pitch, but Ed, protecting the plate, managed to get some wood on it. He looped it into left for a base hit and Cleon

Jones crossed the plate with the winning run in the Mets 4–3 victory.

The Mets were now only four games behind.

After the game the mighty Cubs started to show some cracks in their armor. "That kid in center field," said a fuming Leo Durocher. "Two little fly balls. He just stands there watching one and gives up on the other. It's a disgrace."

"He was just thinking about himself, not the team," said Cub captain Ron Santo of Young's mishaps. "He had a bad day at the bat, so he's got his head down. He's worrying about his batting average and not the team. It's ridiculous. There's no way the Mets can beat us!"

New York ace Tom Seaver started the second game of the series. It was to become one of the most memorable games in the club's history, as the right-hander pitched perfect baseball for 8⅓ innings. There was electricity in the air.

"In the eighth nobody had gotten on base for the Cubs yet," recalls Seaver. "I paused between pitches to look the situation over. Fantastic. They were standing behind the last row of seats all the way down the left-field line and right-field line, and while I stopped to rub the ball they were standing up and yelling their heads off."

In the top of the ninth Cub catcher Randy Hundley led off with a surprise bunt, but Seaver pounced on the ball and threw him out. Next up was Jimmy Qualls, a Cub rookie outfielder who was batting .243 in 47 major-league at-bats. On the first pitch Qualls lined a single to left-center. The perfect game and the no-hitter were lost.

"After Tom gave up that single I went over and talked to him a little longer than I usually would," says Donn Clendenon. "I said, 'Awright Tom, you just fucked up.' He said, 'I fucked up?' I said, 'Yeah Tom, you fucked up. Now let's get the damn thing over with. You pitched a great game and I'm proud of you.' I did that because after you've lost a perfect game it can really blow your mind, so I thought it was best to shake him up a little to kind of bring him down to earth. After the game I just stood there and clapped for him with the fans."

"All the adrenaline that had been running through me drained out," says Tom Seaver of his feelings after Qualls singled. "I felt empty, shocked, numbed. I kept staring into left-center field. I didn't want to believe that the ball had actually fallen safe. I didn't want to believe that I'd come so close to a perfect game and lost it."

The night after Seaver's "imperfect" 4–0 victory, the Cubs salvaged the third game of the series with a 6–2 win. But the Mets had taken two of three and stood only four games back. For the first time in a long time New York city was catching pennant fever.

Despite his club dropping two of three in the first crucial series between the two teams, Club manager Leo Durocher had little respect for the Mets. "There's no way the Mets can go on this way," said Leo. "We won a few games and were eight games ahead of everybody. Then we came back down. The same thing will happen to the Mets. Just wait and see."

Then a writer asked Durocher if those were the real Cubs out there today. Leo, never one to miss an opportunity for a dig, replied, "No, those were the real Mets today."

In the other clubhouse, Mets manager Gil Hodges took everything in stride. "It was a good series," he said. "Any time you take two of three, it's a good series. I'm happy about it. Not satisfied, but happy."

Before leaving New York, Cub third baseman Ron Santo made a statement that would come back to haunt him. "Wait until we get them in Chicago," he told the press. Four days later, after taking two games from the Expos, the Mets travelled to Chicago for another crucial three-game series with the Cubs. The young Mets were anxious to make Ron Santo eat his words.

In the first game of the series the Cubs beat the Mets 1–0 and the Mets dropped 4½ games back. After the game, as if to signal that he had been right, Santo jumped up and clicked his heels. It was the wrong move at the wrong time because it rallied the Mets.

"Our guys really got peeved about Santo doing that," remembers Ed Charles. "He was hot-dogging it and we thought it was a bush thing to do."

"We all thought that Santo was trying to show us up," recalls Don Cardwell. "We just weren't going to be shown up by anybody."

The Mets responded to Santo's actions by taking the next two games from the Cubs, 5–4 and 9–5. The Cubs' lead was cut to 3½ games. "Just another ball game," said Leo Durocher, trying to downplay the Mets' victory in the final game of the series. "Don't forget who's in first place."

"On the bus to the airport after we took the last two games of that series, our spirits were high," says Ed Charles. "I think it was Clendenon who started it by saying , 'Take that, Santo, and shove it!' Hell, these guys are in first place and every time we play them we're winning two out of three. Our confidence was growing. We knew at the start of the season that we were going to win some ball games, but as the season went on our confidence grew and grew because we were beating everybody. It was a gradual thing. It built slowly. But I think after we took that series in Chicago about halfway into the season, we felt to a man that we could win it."

"I'd say it was around that time, about mid-July, when the team felt we could win it all," says Don Cardwell.

At the All-Star break the Amazin' Mets stood only 4½ games behind the first place Cubs. With only a little over two months left in the season the Mets were unbelievably, wonderfully still in the race for the Eastern Division title.

No one could believe what was happening. For the first seven years of their existence the Mets were looked upon by everybody as the "lovable, losing Mets." They were a running joke. But this was a different team. A young team molded by Gil Hodges that believed in itself. A club that saw themselves not as the lovable losers of the past, but as winners. Still, in the back of every Mets fan's mind was the nagging thought that maybe the Mets were playing over their heads. Maybe they were just a flash in the pan. Maybe the whole thing was a fluke.

This seemed to be the case when, shortly after the All-Star break, the Mets went into a tailspin. From July 24 through August 13 the Mets lost 12 of 21 games. On July 30 they were absolutely destroyed by the Astros in a doubleheader at Shea Stadium by the scores of 16–3 and 11–5. In the third inning of the second game, in the midst of a 10–run Astro rally, Gil Hodges made an unprecedented move when left fielder Cleon Jones failed to hustle after an Astro hit. Hodges emerged from the dugout and began walking toward the pitcher's mound. To everyone's surprise, he continued past the mound, past shortstop, and directly to left field where he confronted Cleon Jones. A moment later Jones walked off the field with Hodges. "Sure it was embarrassing," says Jones, looking back on the incident, "but Gil did it with a purpose. He was sending all of us a message. If you didn't hustle and give your best every moment on that field, you were not going to play for him. That's it. I was leading the league in hitting at the time. If he could do that to me, it must've started the other guys thinking, too."

The Mets won three games in a row after the "Jones incident," but then continued to slide. They hit bottom on August 13 when the Astros beat them 8–2 to complete a three-game sweep in the Astrodome. They were now in third place, 9½ behind Chicago.

Gill Hodges had had enough. "It was the middle of August, and we were coming off a 10-day road trip, and Houston had just whipped our asses again," recalls Jerry Grote. "We always had trouble with the Astros. Well, we played like horseshit on the trip, making mental mistakes and all, and when we got back Gil really let us have it. He closed the door to the clubhouse and gave us a serious ass-chewing. It wasn't his style to yell and holler, so when he did you knew he was really, really mad.

"That was really the turning point in the season for us," continues Grote. "After that we took two doubleheaders from San Diego, and that started us up again. From then on there was no stopping us."

"Yeah, after that Houston Series Gil really let us have it," says Ed Charles. "He closed the clubhouse door in New York so the writers couldn't come in, then he chewed us out for about 20 minutes. I mean, he really laced into us. He told us he wouldn't tolerate it if we didn't shape up and that some of the guys wouldn't be back next year and all that. He really got on us. Well, after that he didn't have to say a word the rest of the season. He really shook us up that day. He was so low-key most of the time that when he really chewed us out it shook us up."

In the final month-and-a-half of the season the Mets reeled off winning streaks of six (twice), nine and 10 games, and won 38 of their last 49. Meanwhile the Cubs were doing their yearly tailspin and the Mets moved into first place on September 10, never to move out. Then, on September 24, a year to the day of Gil Hodges' heart attack, the Mets clinched the Eastern Division title when rookie Gary Gentry pitched a 6–0 shutout over the Cardinals. It capped off one of the most exciting and magical comebacks in baseball history. "It was an amazing thing, our second-half drive to the title," says Gary Gentry. "I can't tell you when I realized exactly what we had done. Maybe it's because it was such a long time ago, or maybe it's because at the time so much was happening I just didn't realize it. I'll tell you one thing though. I knew I had to pitch a game on September 24th, and I knew that if we won that game we would win the division. All I was hoping when I got to the ball park that night was that the Cubs had won, because if they'd lost we would have clinched it backdoor. I mean, there were a lot of games left and all we had to do was win one, but I wanted to pitch and win it that night."

Gentry pitched a four-hitter, Donn Clendenon hit two home runs and Ed Charles one, and the Mets became the National League Eastern Division Champions. The race with Chicago was officially over. The young Mets had beaten the veteran Cubs.

"All season long, the rivalry between the Cubs and us had built up," recalls Tom Seaver, "accentuated by Leo Durocher's snide digs at our ability, by Ron Santo's trick of clicking his heels to celebrate each victory, by a few exchanges of brush-back pitches. Yet when we went into Chicago in early October for the final two games, the division championship already clinched, I felt kind of sorry for some of the Cubs. On paper, on sheer physical ability, they had a better club than ours. But we had shown that games aren't won on paper, that it took more than physical ability, that it took concentration and determination and spirit—and, of course, pitching."

During the Mets' late-summer drive to the top they captured the heart of the nation. It was astounding! fantastic! amazing! People who were never interested in baseball before were suddenly walking around with transistor radios pinned to their ears listening to Mets games.

"Everywhere I go, from coast to coast, the Mets have captured the people's interest," said Baseball Commissioner Bowie Kuhn. "It's rising to a crescendo. Even the Customs men ask me, 'How about those Mets?' "

The city of New York was beside itself with excitement. Sure, with the Yankees, Brooklyn Dodgers and New York Giants the city had witnessed more than its fair share of exciting pennant races and World Series. But those teams were expected to win championships. The Mets were a total surprise, 100–to–1 shots when the season started. For all the thrills, excitement and memorable events in the city's baseball history, no team ever captivated New York the way the Mets did in 1969.

"In terms of a catharsis for the population, it's more significant to New York than the circuses were in Rome," said

Henry Cohen, Professor of Urban Affairs and Director of the Center for New York City Affairs at the New School for Social Research.

But the Mets were no longer just New York's team. Indeed, by the time they took the Eastern Division title, they had become America's team. They were like a breath of fresh air. The times were fraught with issues and events that were tearing the country apart: the lingering effects of the assassinations of Martin Luther King, Jr. and Robert Kennedy the year before; the Vietnam War, entering its seventh year with no end in sight and American casualties mounting daily; the peace movement among the nation's young, with its inherent unrest on the streets and college campuses; the rising use of drugs among the nation's young; the civil rights movement and the resulting racial strife causing riots in many of the big cities. All in all it was a year, and indeed a whole decade, that had polarized America.

Then, in the middle of all this confusion, unrest and violence, came the New York Mets. They were unique to the times, a cause that everybody was *for*. It didn't matter if you were black or white, hawk or dove, conservative or liberal, hippie or Marine; the Mets were a cause everybody could relate to. They were the one thing all Americans root for—the underdog.

With each step the Mets took toward the top, their national popularity grew. On September 5, nearly three weeks before they clinched the division title, they were featured on the cover of *Time Magazine*. In over six decades of publication, through more than 3,000 issues, baseball had been the subject of *Time's* cover only 36 times. Thirty-five of those covers pictured individual stars such as Mel Ott, Joe DiMaggio and Jackie Robinson. The 1969 New York Mets were the only baseball team in history to appear on its cover. And they did it before they'd won anything!

Shortly after the *Time* cover came out, Gil Hodges and the Mets pitching staff appeared in a national television commercial for Vitalis hair tonic. Hurlers Tom Seaver, Jerry Koosman, Nolan Ryan, Don Cardwell, Cal Koonce and Gary Gentry are standing shoulder to shoulder, in uniform, facing manager Hodges. "Now, listen to me," says Hodges. "The commissioner has given a direct order. Anyone suspected of using grease on his hair for the purposes of throwing a greaseball shall be immediately removed from the game. Everybody hear that?" The pitchers nod as Hodges walks down the line, inspecting each man's hair as he goes. He comes to rookie Gary Gentry, who appears uncomfortable. Looking him over, the manager walks behind him, removes Gentry's cap, and rubs his hair. "Grease!" says Hodges. "Gentry, you're the first pitcher ever sent to the showers without throwing a ball!" As the rookie walks dejectedly toward the showers, Hodges calls his name and tosses him a bottle of "greaseless" Vitalis.

In early October, Buddha records released an album entitled "The Amazin' Mets." The team had cut the disc the morning after clinching the Eastern Division title. According to Jerry Koosman: "Most of us were still drunk from the night before. And if that wasn't bad enough, when we arrived at the studio at 9:30 in the morning we saw that the record company had provided us with as much champagne as we could drink." Needless to say, the club was pretty much "in the bag" during the recording session, a fact to which the finished product bears witness. On the record the team belts out a dozen inspirational songs such as "You Gotta Have Heart" and the like. Incredibly, the album sold over 50,000 copies; certainly not a gold record, but considering it was quite possibly the worst singing ever put on vinyl, that sales total was, like the team itself, absolutely amazing. Today the record is a rare and valuable collector's item.

Throughout the nation, Mets fever was spreading like wildfire. On television and radio newscasts around the country, the scores of Mets games were often featured in the news portion of the show. Sportscasters and sportswriters in many of the major league cities were devoting just as much air time and newspaper space, if not more, to coverage of the Mets as they were to their respective home teams. By the time the Mets stood ready to meet the Western Division Champion Atlanta Braves for the pennant in the first-ever League Championship Series, they had become America's home team.

It was felt by most experts that in order for the Mets to beat the Braves in the best-of-five series, their superb pitching would have to silence Atlanta's booming bats. The Braves had some genuine sock in their lineup with Orlando Cepeda, Rico Carty, Felipe Alou and the great Henry Aaron. What's more, the Mets had lost their most potent offensive weapon, Donn Clendenon, who had sustained a shoulder injury. For the first time all season long the Mets' pitching caved in. It didn't matter, however, because the offense came to the rescue by scoring 27 runs in three games and the Mets swept the Braves to take the National League pennant.

"The club was a little tight before that first game in Atlanta," says Donn Clendenon. "Now my shoulder was hurt so Gil said he was going to try and keep me out. So before the first game I went into the clubhouse and said, "Awright you son of a bitches, I'm not out there now so show me what you can do without me. I know I'm the key to this club, but see if you can win without me in there.' Of course I said it for a laugh just to try and loosen them up a little bit. But the kids, they didn't need me for that series. Their bats just came alive."

In the first game Mets ace Tom Seaver gave up five runs by the fifth inning, an unusually bad outing for him. But the offense came up with nine runs for a 9–5 victory. "I was more tense than usual, and more nervous," said Seaver of his performance in the first game. "It's a progressive thing that happens to me all the time, except that the tension dissipates itself usually after my first pitch. But today my mental state led me to rush my pitching motion physically. My hips were more open when I was throwing the ball, and my arm dropped lower. Jerry came out to the mound several times and told me to get my arm back higher. It just seemed that I couldn't throw that many good pitches in a row. Some of them were good, and I guess that's what made me keep my sanity. The crux of the whole thing, though, was that I just felt more nervous than usual.''

In the second game of the series the Mets piled up a 9–1 lead after four innings, and it looked like smooth sailing for Jerry Koosman. But the southpaw was knocked out of the box in the bottom of the fourth when he gave up five runs with two men out. "I wasn't really that nervous, I think I just got tired," recalls Koosman of that game. "It was extremely hot, over 90 degrees, and I think I got just a little worn out by the time I gave up those runs." Relievers Ron Taylor and Tug McGraw held the Braves the rest of the way and Cleon Jones blasted a two-run homer to seal the Mets' 11–6 victory.

Rookie Gary Gentry pitched the third game for the Mets, and things started badly when Hank Aaron blasted a two-run homer off him in the first. "That was the only game that season where I was a little more nervous than usual," recalls Gary Gentry. "Seaver and Koosman had both gotten their asses kicked in the first two games, so I figure I'm going to go out there and show them how to do it. I start out real good and then I'm facing Hank Aaron. With the count 1-and-1 I threw him a curveball that just dropped off the table. It really fooled him and now I have two strikes on him.

"At the time a friend of mine was watching the game on TV and he told me that after that curveball the announcer says, 'That was a beautiful pitch, but sometimes a young pitcher will come back with the same pitch and you can't do that with a hitter like Aaron.' Well, that announcer should have been talking to me because that's just what I did, and Aaron hits the son of a bitch past the center field flag pole." Gentry smiles and shakes his head at the memory. "Who the hell did I think I was throwing to? Some rookie?"

Gentry got in trouble again in the second when the Braves put men on second and third with nobody out and Rico Carty at the plate. "Rico Carty couldn't hit me from yesterday," says Gentry. "He's one of those bulky guys so I'm jamming him with the ball and he keeps fouling them off. After he fouled off the third or fourth pitch I noticed that he changed his stance and opened up a little. Grote noticed it and wanted to throw to a different location, but I shook him off because I still wanted to go inside. So I threw him an inside fastball and he rifles the son of a bitch just foul down the left-field line. It hit off the left-field wall, and the next thing I know Hodges is coming out to the mound to take me out of the game. I'm the only pitcher I know who was ever taken out of a game because of a foul ball. So there I am sitting on the bench in the second inning on the day I'm going to show everyone how good I am because Seaver and Koosman got their asses kicked in the first two games."

Nolan Ryan came in to relieve Gentry, struck out Carty and retired the next two hitters to escape the inning without giving up a run. "Gil knew exactly what he was doing when he brought Ryan in in that situation," says Jerry Grote. "The Braves had a shot at putting the game away early; so Gil just didn't want to stop them, he wanted to absolutely over-power them and blow them away. Ryan, with his stuff, was the only man in the bullpen capable of that. He blew away Carty and just shut down the Braves."

The Braves scored two runs off Ryan later when Orlando Cepeda blasted a two-run homer in the top of the fifth to give Atlanta a 4–3 lead. In the home half of the inning, however, Ryan singled and third baseman Wayne Garrett, who had hit one home run all season, blasted one into the right-field bullpen to put the Mets on top 5–4. Ryan was unhittable the rest of the way, and the Mets scored two more runs to take the National League pennant with a 7–4 victory. Tom Seaver led the stampede to the mound as the young Mets celebrated their victory. Gil Hodges leaned over into the box seats and kissed his wife Joan. Only 72 days prior to the Mets winning the pennant, Neil Armstrong had walked on the moon. But somehow that paled in comparison to the Mets taking the National League title.

NOW THE METS WERE TO FACE EARL WEAVER'S BAL-
timore Orioles in the World Series. Most experts predicted
that the O's, who had won 109 games—nine more than the
Mets—in the regular season, would make short work of the
upstart Mets. Many people considered this Baltimore team
one of the greatest clubs in baseball history. Their potent
offense boasted Frank Robinson, Brooks Robinson, Boog
Powell, Davey Johnson and Don Buford. They had pitching
to match the Mets in starters Mike Cuellar, Dave McNally and
Jim Palmer, and in the bullpen Dick Hall, Eddie Watt and
Pete Richert were all coming off banner years. Their defense
was also outstanding with Mark Belanger at short, Paul Blair
in center and the great Brooks Robinson at third.

Despite the overwhelming odds, the young Mets were
confident they could win. "You know, we picked up the
paper before the Series started and in all the comparisons,
position by position, we were a minus all the way down,"
says Bud Harrelson. "We said, 'Who cares? What, are they
going to beat us in the newspaper? Big deal.' We knew we
could win."

From the start of the Series the veteran Orioles tried to
intimidate the young Mets. "I remember we had just finished
taking batting practice when a pitcher on their club named
Jim Hardin came walking up to me," recalls Jerry Koosman.
"He says, 'What are you guys doing here?' I said, 'What do
you mean?' He says, 'You guys don't belong in the Series.
Man for man and statistically you don't belong on the same
field with us.' Well, I just shook my head and walked away
from him. When I got to the clubhouse I got everybody's
attention and I told them what Hardin had said. The lights
went out for the Orioles shortly after that. Nobody was
going to intimidate us, not verbally or otherwise."

In the bottom of the first inning of the first game in
Baltimore, Don Buford led off with a home run off Met
starter Tom Seaver. The ball just made it over the right-field
wall as Ron Swoboda leapt to try to snare it.

"I came inside with a fastball," says Seaver of the home-run pitch, "a good fastball. Buford got his bat around quick and lifted a fly ball to right field, an easy fly ball, I thought at first. Then I saw Ron Swoboda fading back, and back, and back, and I wondered what's going on? And then I saw Ron leap and saw the ball sail over his glove and saw it bounce on the far side of the fence. I couldn't believe it. I had faced one batter in my first World Series game, and I had given up one home run." ("Swoboda should have caught that fucking ball," says Donn Clendenon; "he just miss-timed his jump.")

"When Buford was rounding second on that home run he turns to me and says, 'You ain't seen nothin' yet,' " recalls Bud Harrelson. "And I'm thinking, what the hell is he talking about? This is only the first inning of the first game. Hell, he ain't seen nothin' yet either. There's no question they tried to intimidate us, but you just couldn't. We were too confident."

The Orioles went on to win the game 4–1 behind Mike Cuellar and took a one-game lead in the Series. Baltimore did not, however, dominate the Mets. Still, many people took the Oriole victory as a sign that the Mets' fragile bubble had finally burst. They couldn't have been more wrong. "It was just nerves that first game," says Donn Clendenon. "I think everybody was a little tight, even myself. I found myself overswinging and I knew I had to make some adjustments."

"With all the media coverage and attention leading up to that first game, it's a natural thing to feel a little nervous," says Ed Charles. "I know I felt nervous but I couldn't let it show. Being the senior member of the team if I showed I was a little tight it might have affected the younger players. So I was trying to relax the pressurized atmosphere in the club-house. It's like a field leader in a battle. Although he's scared shitless he's going to get killed, he can't show that to the men or how are they going to feel? But I think that first game was just a game where you had to get over that initial nervousness of being in the Series, and I knew we would then come back and play our type of game."

"After we lost that first game the clubhouse was a little quiet," says Jerry Grote. "Then Gil walked in and said, 'Hey you guys, you played good out there. There's nothing to hang your head about. We know now we can beat them.' Well, coming from Gil you just believed it, because at that point everybody on the club had total and complete confidence in him. Then Tom Seaver stood up and said, "Boys, we found out something today. If that's the best they've got there's no way they're going to beat us. No way.' "

"We came into the clubhouse after the game more confident than when we had left it," recalls Tom Seaver. "Somebody, I think it was Clendenon, yelled out, 'Dammit, we can beat these guys!' And we believed it. A team knows if they've been badly beaten or outplayed. And we felt we hadn't been. The feeling wasn't that we had lost, but hey, we nearly won that game. We hadn't been more than a hit or two from turning it around. It hit us like a ton of bricks. I tell you, that was the chemistry we had on the '69 Mets, these sudden surges of everybody thinking alike."

"Yeah, the Orioles tried to intimidate us," remembers Donn Clendenon. "But they couldn't do it. After that first game I said to the guys, 'Let me tell you something. Seaver didn't have shit out there today and they barely beat us. If that's all they have we're going to beat them the next four straight.'

"The next day during batting practice their center fielder, Paul Blair, walks up to me and says, 'You guys are in way over your heads.' I just turned to him and said, 'Paul, we're gonna beat you today and then you have to come back to New York, and let me tell you something, you guys are gonna leave New York with your fuckin' heads between your legs.' "

Ed Charles had an experience similar to Clendenon's with Oriole coach George Bamberger. "Bamby was walking by me before the second game and he was laughing and gave me a wink as he went by," recalls Charles. "I said, 'You better wipe that grin off your face because you guys won the only game you're going to win.' "

"That first game didn't affect us that much," says coach Rube Walker. "Gil never doubted we could win it all and he made the players feel like that. We didn't lose any of our confidence."

"Even after losing that first game we were confident we could win," recalls Cleon Jones. "that was the key to our club, our confidence level. I remember that after we beat the Braves in the playoffs I had a chance to speak to Hank Aaron and he was just amazed by how much confidence we had in ourselves. 'I've been in baseball a long time,' he said, 'but I've never seen a team with the kind of confidence you guys have. Not just as individuals, but in each other, too.'

"After we lost that first game some of us went out to dinner that night," Jones continues, "and at the next table some guy is going on about how the Orioles are going to sweep the Mets and how the Mets didn't belong in the Series, and all that. I was getting pretty mad listening to him, so I turned around and said, 'You don't know me, but I'll bet you anything that the Mets win it.' I wasn't serious about the bet, I was just mad. So the guy says, "Sure, I'll bet.' I said, 'Okay, what do you want to bet, $10,000, $20,000?' Well the guy looked at me like I was crazy, so he goes and asks somebody who we are. He comes back to the table and says, 'So you guys are the Mets.' I said 'Yeah, we're the Mets and we're gonna win. You think the Orioles can beat us? They can't beat us. We may have lost today, but we're gonna win tomorrow and we're gonna win the whole thing!' That's the way we all felt. We were confident we could take them."

Over two decades later Oriole center fielder Paul Blair denies that the veteran Orioles tried to intimidate the Mets. "No," he says, "we didn't try to intimidate them. Look, nobody gets into the World Series that can't play the game of baseball. That whole Series was just an unfortunate thing for us. I'll tell you one thing, the Mets had confidence in themselves, and when you saw the kind of plays they were making you couldn't help feeling like something special was going on.''

In game two left-hander Jerry Koosman started for the Mets and pitched six innings of no-hit ball as the Mets defeated the Orioles 2–1 to tie the Series. "My goal at that point in my life was to pitch a no-hitter in the World Series and get a hit every time up," says Koosman. "Well, I got a hit every time up and I'm really trying my best to pitch a no-hitter, but Paul Blair broke it up with a single up the middle in the seventh. I almost did it, though."

When Blair singled the Mets were leading 1–0 on Donn Clendenon's first home run of the Series. Blair then stole second and scored on Brooks Robinson's single to tie the game. But in the top of the ninth Ed Charles singled and Jerry Grote came to the plate. From the dugout Gil Hodges flashed the hit-and-run sign, and it worked perfectly as Grote singled and Ed Charles ended up on third base. The move caught the Orioles off-guard as Hodges thought it would. Says Jerry Grote: "Gil always said to me, 'Jerry, you're a good hit-and-run man, so please check with the coach on every pitch when there's a runner on because you'll never known when I'll hit-and-run with you.' That was a perfect spot for it and it set up what turned out to be the winning run."

Al Weis followed with another single and the Mets took a 2–1 lead into the bottom of the ninth. Koosman quickly got the first two outs, but then walked the next two Orioles, bringing Brooks Robinson, one of the game's most dangerous clutch hitters, to the plate. Hodges took Koosman out of the game and brought in ace right-handed reliever Ron Taylor.

"I knew I had to get Robinson out," says Taylor, "if not, we might have gone back to New York two games down. It was the toughest one-on-one test I ever had."

Taylor ran the count to 3-and-2 on Robinson, and on the next pitch the Oriole third baseman ripped a hard ground ball to third. Veteran Ed Charles was there, and he made an excellent play on a difficult ball. "The tough thing about that play was that it was an in-between hop," he says. "I couldn't move in to field it cleanly, and I couldn't back up fast enough to get the good hop. I knew once I caught it that it was too late to get the runner at third; but knowing Robinson was a slower runner, I had plenty of time to get him at first to end the game."

The Series, now tied at a game a piece, moved back to New York, and the Mets were very happy to get out of Baltimore. "They gave us a lot of shit down there," says Grote. "All the tickets they gave us were shitty so our wives and everybody had to sit way the hell down the right-field line. I mean way down by the flag pole. Everything about the place was ridiculous. Hell, after we split in Baltimore our only concern was winning the next three in New York so we didn't have to go back to that damn rat hole."

The third game pitted Met Rookie Gary Gentry against Baltimore ace Jim Palmer. Gentry pitched effectively for six innings in the Mets' 5–3 victory, and even helped his own cause with a two-run double off Palmer in the second inning. Everybody was surprised by Gentry's hit except the rookie pitcher himself. "What most people don't realize is that in high school and college the pitchers are usually the best athletes on the team, both pitching and hitting," says Gentry. "Of course, when you get into pro ball you only hit every four days or so and your hitting suffers. But I knew I could hit and I figured Jim Palmer was going to be in love with his fastball and that's all he'd throw me. So I went up there figuring he's going to throw me a fastball and I'm going to knock the shit out if it, and that's what I did."

Another hero in the game was Met center fielder Tommie Agee. After going hitless the first two games, Agee led off game three with a homer on Jim Palmer's fourth pitch. "I couldn't believe it," says Palmer, looking back. "At that point in my career I had pitched over 500 innings in the big leagues and had never given up a lead-off homer. I couldn't do it in Cleveland in August. No. I had to do it in a World Series game.''

But Agee's heroics didn't stop with his home run. Later in the game he made not one, but two, of the greatest catches in World Series history to crush two Baltimore rallies. The first catch came in the top of the fourth with the Mets leading 3–0. The Orioles had runners on first and second with two outs and Elrod Hendricks at the plate. Hendricks drove a Gentry pitch deep into the gap in left-center. When it left the bat it looked like a sure two-base hit. Then, coming out of nowhere and running at top speed, Agee made a spectacular back-handed stab of the liner on the warning track. The ball was sticking out of the top of his glove like an ice cream cone. The catch saved two runs. "There's no way I thought he was going to catch that ball," says Bud Harrelson. "I was already set in my cut-off position, but Tommie came up with it. It was a spectacular catch."

"It was a great catch," remembers left fielder Cleon Jones, who was right next to Agee when he made the grab. "People don't realize how much ground Tommie could cover. I was not surprised that he made the play because I knew how good he was."

Ironically, Agee's catch was difficult only because, according to Gentry, Agee was out of position to begin with. Says Gentry: "We went over the whole Oriole lineup before the game, and we figured Hendricks for a left-handed, dead pull hitter. So our strategy was to pitch him away and play him away, toward center or left-center, to take away his strength."

"So I threw one low and away like I was supposed to and he drove it toward left-center like he was supposed to. I turned around figuring it was nothing. He hit the ball well but it's not a home run and we're supposed to be playing him there anyway. Well, I turn around and no one's there. Agee's over toward right-center and Cleon's all the way over in left field. So Agee runs over there and makes this spectacular catch and becomes a national hero. I didn't say anything then, but I was thinking that if he doesn't make the catch I'm going to be pissed as shit because he's out of position, and we went over all this before the game.''

Gentry pitched effectively through the first six innings of game three, and got the first two batters in the top of the seventh. Then he walked three Orioles in a row. Hodges took the rookie hurler out of the game and brought in fastballer Nolan Ryan to face Paul Blair. At the time many people second-guessed Hodges about bringing in Ryan. Although the young Texan threw harder than anybody else in baseball, he was wild and constantly in trouble with walks. The question was, why would Hodges bring in a wild young pitcher with the bases loaded late in the game and only a two-run lead. But Gil Hodges knew exactly what he was doing. He was taking a calculated risk that paid off. ''It took guts to do that, but Gil knew what he was doing,'' says Bud Harrelson. ''Let's face it, Nolan Ryan, at that stage in his career, was wild an awful lot so he had been in that same exact situation a number of times before. A lot of times he'd start the inning by walking three guys, then strike out the side. So Hodges brings him in there with the money on the line and he does the job. Gil knew that of all our pitchers, Ryan was the one who had pitched in that situation most often.''

On Ryan's third pitch Blair drove a fastball deep into the gap in right-center and Agee was off and running again. This time he made a diving, sliding catch on the warning track to save three runs for his second spectacular grab of the day. Ryan retired the Orioles in the next two innings and the Mets had a 5–3 victory and a two-games-to-one lead in the Series.

After the game a writer asked Baltimore manager Earl Weaver if he thought the Mets were a team of destiny. ''No,'' replied Earl, ''they're a team with some fine defensive outfielders.''

That night, after his brilliant game, Tommie Agee had trouble sleeping. ''I kept dreaming about the catches,'' recalls Agee, "and I kept waking up screaming. In my dreams, I kept missing the catches."

The fourth game pitted Mets ace Tom Seaver against Baltimore left-hander Mike Cuellar. First basemen Donn Clendenon blasted his second home run of the Series in the second inning, and Seaver, pitching effectively, took a 1–0 lead into the ninth. but with one man out Frank Robinson and Boog Powell singled, and once again third baseman Brooks Robinson came to the plate in a clutch situation. Robinson hit a sinking line drive to right field and Ron Swoboda came charging in, making one of the greatest catches in World Series history. He dove, slid along the grass and came up with the ball. "There's no way I ever thought Swoboda was going to catch that ball," recalls Gary Gentry, who was watching from the bench. "When it was hit it looked like he didn't have a chance. But then he caught it and came up throwing, which was a real heads up play, especially for Ron. Let's face it, Ron was never known for his outstanding defensive abilities, but he came up big in that game."

"I watched, fascinated by the race between Ron and the ball," says Tom Seaver. "I should have been moving somewhere, backing up third or backing up home, but my fielding instincts weren't working. Besides, I wasn't certain whether the ball was going to go through or be caught or be trapped, and I didn't know for sure where I should be moving. The ball started to sink toward the ground, and Ron left his feet and dove and jabbed out his glove backhanded. The ball hit the glove. It stuck."

"I was going for it all the way," says Swoboda. "To be a good outfielder you have to be aggressive, and after I came up with it my only concern was getting the ball in because I knew Frank Robinson would be tagging from third."

"When Ron first came up he couldn't catch a ball with a bucket," recalls a smiling Cleon Jones. "But Ron really worked on his outfield play. He worked as hard as anybody

I've ever seen, and it paid off when he made that catch in the World Series."

"It was a great catch, granted," says Donn Clendenon of Swoboda's grab, "but from a pure baseball standpoint he was a dumb son of a bitch for trying for it in that situation. If the ball gets by him two runs score and we're behind. Obviously the right play was to take it on the hop. As it turned out Ron made one hell of a catch, but it was a dumb-ass play."

"The Mets had something special going for them," says Oriole center fielder Paul Blair. "We just couldn't do anything to overcome them. You take Swoboda's catch. He was not what you would call a good defensive outfielder. If I fell out of the sky he couldn't catch me, but then he comes up with that spectacular grab. The Mets just kept coming up with the big play at the right time."

On Swoboda's catch Frank Robinson tagged up from third to tie the game. Seaver then retired the next two hitters, and after the Mets went down in order in the bottom of the ninth, the game went into extra innings.

In the bottom of the tenth inning, with the score tied at one, Jerry Grote led off for the Mets with a short flyball to left field. It should have been the first out of the inning, but Oriole left fielder Don Buford lost the ball in the bright sky. At first he backed up, then, realizing his mistake, starting running in. The ball dropped between Buford and shortstop Mark Belanger, and Grote slid into second with a double. Hodges sent Rod Gaspar in to run for Grote. Oriole reliever Dick Hall then intentionally walked Al Weis, who had reached base seven times in the first three games. With Tom Seaver due up, Hodges sent in a backup catcher J.C. Martin, a left-handed batter, to pinch-hit against the right-handed Hall. Oriole skipper Earl Weaver countered this move by bringing in lefty Pete Richert.

Martin's orders were to bunt the potential winning run over to third with Tommie Agee coming up next. On the first pitch Martin laid down a perfect bunt. Richert came racing in and fired the ball toward first. Suddenly the ball was rolling into right field. It had hit off Martin's wrist. Gaspar never broke stride and crossed the plate with the winning run.

After the game replays showed that Martin had been running inside the baseline and could have been called out, nullifying the run. But the Orioles lodged no protest and the Mets took a three-games-to-one lead into the fifth game of the Series.

The pitching match-up for game five was Jerry Koosman for the Mets versus Oriole right-hander Dave McNally. The Orioles jumped off to a 3–0 lead in the third inning when pitcher McNally hit a two-run homer, followed by a sole blast from Frank Robinson.

Says Jerry Koosman: "After Robinson hit that home run I went into the dugout and said, 'That's it guys, they aren't going to get any more runs. I'll hold them. Let's get some runs on the board.' And to show the Orioles I meant it, the next time Robinson came up I threw at him. It was a fastball and it hit him in the leg, but the umpire called it a foul ball. I wanted to let Robinson know we weren't going to be intimidated."

In the sixth inning of that game, with Baltimore still leading 3–0, one of the most interesting incidents in World Series history occurred. With nobody out, Oriole pitcher Dave McNally threw a curveball in the dirt near the feet of lead-off hitter Cleon Jones. The umpire called it a ball, but Jones claimed it had hit him on the foot. At the time, Donn Clendenon was the on-deck hitter. "I wasn't even sure it hit him," recalls Clendenon. "All I knew was that we needed base runners. So I told the umpire: 'You have to realize one thing; they polish our shoes every night. If that ball hit him you're going to have some polish on the goddam ball. It don't take a Ph.D. to figure that out.' "

Meanwhile, in the Met dugout, Gil Hodges was thinking the same thing. "That ball came into the dugout and I caught it," remembers Jerry Koosman. "I'm looking at it and Gil says, 'Jerry, let me see that ball.' Gil took it and turned it over and found the shoe polish. He took it out to the umpire right away. The whole thing didn't take more than five seconds. The umpire then reversed his call and awarded Cleon first base. Now, in the back of some people's minds they might be thinking that Gil hit it on his own shoe. But that didn't happen. It actually hit Cleon on the foot.''

"That's where Gil's reputation really helped us,'' says Bud Harrelson. "You know, if you're a real crazy manager who's always screaming and you go out there, the ump says, 'So what. How do I know that's the right ball?' but when Hodges walks out there, the ump says, 'This guy's a real gentleman, he's honest, he doesn't rant or rave and scream at me and call me names. He only comes out when he knows he's right.' So what's the umpire going to do? Call Gill Hodges a liar?''

Naturally when Jones was given first base, Oriole manager Earl Weaver came running out of the dugout and began arguing. McNally joined in with Weaver, but it was to no avail. As Weaver trotted back to the dugout and the umpire took up his position behind the plate, McNally yelled, "Jesus Christ, we never get a break!''

Donn Clendenon, waiting to hit, replied, "Just go out there and pitch the goddam ball!'' McNally pitched, and on a 2-and-2 count, Clendenon hit his third home run of the Series, bringing the Mets to within one run.

In the bottom of the seventh Met second baseman Al Weis, who to that point in his eight-year big-league career had hit a total of six home runs, but was hitting over .400 in the Series, blasted a shot over the left field wall to tie the game.

"At that point the Orioles were a defeated team,'' says Donn Clendenon. "You could see it in their posture. Their shoulders just slumped. They were a great team, but after Al hit that homer they knew they couldn't win. It buried them.''

In the bottom of the eighth the Mets scored two more runs on doubles by Cleon Jones and Ron Swoboda and an error by Oriole first baseman Boog Powell. They took a 5–3 lead into the ninth, only three outs away from the summit. Koosman walked Frank Robinson to lead off the inning, but Boog Powell grounded into a force play for the first out. Brooks Robinson then flied out, bringing up second baseman Davey Johnson as the Orioles' final hope.

Two decades later a number of Met players recall the end of that game and the miracle year.

JERRY KOOSMAN

All I was trying to do in that last inning was throw strikes. We're ahead 5–3 and I didn't want to walk anybody. If they were going to score off me it had to be a sole home run. In my own mind I kept telling myself just throw strikes. I was so nervous and getting so excited already, and the crowd is on its feet.

You have to remember that mentally you're not normal at that point, so when Davey Johnson hit that last fly ball to left, it seemed to me like it might be out of here. During the season when a hit like that leaves the bat you know it's not a home run, just a long fly ball, but with all that excitement and adrenalin flowing, you're thinking it might be gone. But it wasn't.

When Cleon got under it I'm sure he felt the same nervousness and excitement going through him. I was just praying, saying to myself, "Cleon, just stay loose and catch the ball with relaxed hands, and don't let it drop!" Well, he caught it and went down on one knee and . . . it was just . . . I can't explain it . . . your mind is just flooding with excitement. Pandemonium breaks out. What an experience. Chills go through your body. It's a dream come true. Even after you win it's like you're still dreaming.

Pretty soon all the fans start coming on the field. You're so excited and all of a sudden you get a little scared because you don't know what they're going to do. I hung on to my glove and cap because I'm already thinking they're going in my trophy case. People are grabbing at you, and to work your way into the clubhouse was really scary. People were falling over the dugout roof, jumping off, falling on the steps and lying there. I remember going down the clubhouse steps and they were lying there three and four people thick. I stepped on one guy and my spikes went into his leg, but you couldn't walk unless you stepped on people. I finally made it to the clubhouse and I was so excited and grateful that it was over with. I was all tight in my throat. I couldn't talk. It was just your eyes did all the talking for you. A lot of the guys were that way, hugging each other, but so overcome they couldn't talk.

CLEON JONES

When that last fly ball came out to me I knew we were going to be World Champions. I wasn't nervous at all as it came down, although it did seem like it took forever to get to me. I went down on one knee after the catch just to make sure. After I caught it I paused for a second and then started racing for the clubhouse. I knew the fans would be pouring onto the field and I wanted to make sure I held on to that ball.

It was really a special year for me, because Tommie [Agee] and I did it together. We had grown up together, played ball together, and both had dreams of making the big leagues. Well, we both made it, and then to be together on a World Championship team: hell, it can't get any better than that. Even in your wildest dreams you can't visualize something like that.

BUD HARRELSON

That final out went over my head toward Cleon and I knew he was going to catch it, and I said to myself, "Oh my God, we're World Champions."

I didn't even stop at the mound, because it had been mayhem when we clinched the division against St. Louis. They went absolutely crazy at Shea. Then when we beat the Braves for the pennant they practically killed us. They were tearing at our shirts and hats. At the end of the Series I headed straight for the dugout as fast as I could. There was a stream of people coming over the top of the dugout, like a waterfall. It was pretty scary. I got to the clubhouse and got my father in there, then opened the door and kissed my mom. Then I just sat by my locker. Things were pretty crazy in the clubhouse, but I wasn't running around or anything. I was sitting there and the only thing I could think about was the World Series ring we were going to get. That ring would signify to everybody, when they looked at it, that I was part of an historic team.

TOM SEAVER

Koosman walked Frank Robinson in the ninth, then Powell grounded out. Brooks Robinson flied out. Davey Johnson hit a gentle fly to left. Cleon caught it with his body in a low crouch and then touched one knee to the grass for an instant.

'We won! We won!' I couldn't say it often enough.

Everywhere there was champagne, running down my back, even on the head of John Lindsay, the Mayor of New York, who was running for reelection. There was a crush of reporters and cameras. All the world wanted to know about the amazing Mets.

I remember going off in a corner of the room with my own bottle of champagne, leaning against a sink with Rube Walker, and watching everything. I had what I wanted. We had won it all. Lord, it was good . . . .

Of all the thrills I had while playing in New York, certainly the biggest and most memorable one was winning the World Series in 1969. Regardless of what you do individually, the biggest goal is always the team goal; to win it all together, and that's what we did. That team had great chemistry and we all worked together toward a common goal and achieved it. To be able to share that with all the guys—Koos, Cleon, Buddy, Jerry, Swoboda, all of them—was great. It's something they'll never be able to take away from us.

ED CHARLES

It's an impossible feeling to describe. The ball gets hit to left and you're holding back until Cleon catches it. Then you explode. All this jubilation comes pouring out. You release it in one big, broad, happy, joyous expression. Then all the people come pouring onto the field, and you race for the dugout and try to get into the clubhouse before you maybe get hurt.

I'll tell you, it was some year. We were a team of destiny. I really believe that. We had talent, but so many things happened that year it was just unbelievable.

It was so sweet for me because I had waited a long time. I spent 10 years in the minors before I got my break with the Athletics. I was a 30-year-old rookie. Then I came to the Mets in 1968, and I figured in spring training of '69 that it was going to be my last year. I was going on 36 years old and had played eight years in the majors. So for me it was the best way to end my playing career. You can't do any better than going out a World Champion.

JERRY GROTE

I remember thinking that I better get off the field before I get mauled by the fans. When that ball hit I knew we were going to be World Champions, so my next thought was, okay, now let's get the hell out of here.

Actually, winning the World Series was great, but I'll tell you, after winning the division and the pennant, we were all kind of partied out.

What really sticks out in my mind about winning it was the parade they gave us. The day of the parade the cops shut down all the entrances to the Grand Central Parkway so our motorcade could have clear sailing from Shea Stadium into Manhattan. You know what New York traffic is like, and you know how pissed off New Yorkers get when they have to sit in it. Traffic was backed for miles at the entrances to the highway, but the people didn't care. They were just waving and cheering and honking their horns as we went by. It was unbelievable. One of the most amazing things I've ever seen. Boy, let me tell you New York was one happy city.

AL WEIS

That was the first World Series the Mets ever played in and we won it, and being such underdogs made it really special. The Series I had was just fantastic for me. Not many people know this, but I was originally born and raised in New York, about 15 minutes from Shea. Coming back to play in a series in front of your hometown crowd was a big thrill. You just never think that something that fantastic can happen to you.

Some people say it was a miracle, but I don't think so, not at all. We had some good ballplayers on that club. Some players had outstanding years and some had average ones, and when you combine that with the kind of pitching we had, we were a solid ball club.

I think the main thing we had going for us was confidence. Gil instilled that in us. We were winning games where we were losing going into the ninth inning. But somehow we always knew we were going to win no matter how many runs we were down.

GARY GENTRY

That was my rookie year: I was only 23, and I don't think what we did really hit me until much later on. You know, I went out there and pitched every fourth day, then I pitched in the post-season, and I just got swept along by the whole thing. It was one of the greatest experiences of my life, but I really didn't realize how wonderful it was until some time had passed.

Later on in my career I went through a lot of shit. I hurt my arm and it was misdiagnosed by the doctors, so what was a minor injury at the time turned into a major one that ended my career. I had a lot of bitterness and I felt used. It was very frustrating and very hard on me mentally. I went through a lot of shit before I came to grips with it. But I'll tell you something. Being able to look at that World Championship ring, and knowing I was an important part of a great team, that makes it all worthwhile.

DONN CLENDENON

When Cleon caught that ball for the final out, my only thought was, it's over. I was tired. During the ticker-tape parade I went as far as city hall then disappeared. I just wanted to sleep. I couldn't go back to my apartment because people were waiting for me there, so some friends of mine arranged for me to get the penthouse at the Essex House Hotel. I went there and slept for almost two days.

It was really an amazing year. I think the thing I remember most was seeing these young ballplayers reach the confidence level they reached. You could walk into our clubhouse and see it in their eyes. Nobody was going to beat us.

It was a great ball club. You want to know why it was great? Because we had a lot of guys with no super talent, but they started to mesh and do everything in their capacity to win. Everybody put out 110 percent all the time. It was a collective team effort. We all made our contributions.

You don't win 100 games and a World Championship on luck. That team came together as a unit and believed it was a natural winner. We didn't give a damn if you were 10 runs ahead; we totally believed—and this is no pie-in-the-sky bull-shit—we totally believed we would overcome that deficit and win. And it all goes back to Gil Hodges. He never wavered. He made us believe we were winners.

*   *   *

THE MET'S DRIVE TO THE 1969 WORLD CHAMPION-ship is frequently referred to as "The Miracle of '69," as if their victory were the result of some divine intervention. Or perhaps a fluke. Neither is true. The Mets won on steady team play, and on overwhelmingly strong pitching. "Miracle, my eye," says Tom Seaver. "What happened was that a lot of good young players suddenly jelled and matured at once. The chemistry on that ball club was a beautiful thing to feel and to see in action. Everybody had to contribute something because we weren't that powerful, and everybody did contribute."

The popularity of the 1969 Mets peaked with their victory over the Orioles in the World Series, and remained high throughout that winter. "We were pretty popular," says Bud Harrelson with a smile. "The nation wanted to see us."

"There are those sweet spots in time when something happens unlike anything that's ever happened before," says Tug McGraw. "My best memory isn't really a game; it's the feeling that that moment was shared by the whole country—the whole country was Mets fans."

"It was a colossal thing that they did," said a proud Gil Hodges of his team. "These young men showed that you can realize the most impossible dream of all."

When the team appeared on the Ed Sullivan Show after the Series to do a song from their "hit" record, the studio audience roared with delight. Six members of the club were booked into a Las Vegas hotel for two weeks as a singing act. All through the winter members of the team were in demand as guest speakers at functions and dinners around the nation. Many Mets were given special days and parades when they returned to their home towns for the off-season. And still others appeared as guests on nationally televised talk shows. America couldn't get enough of the Mets.

The ticker-tape parade New York City gave its World Champions on October 20, 1969, was the largest and wildest in the city's history. Joyous fans dumped over 1,254 tons of paper on the Mets motorcade—more than had fallen on any President, war hero, or anyone else in history. "It was absolutely intoxicating," remembers pitcher Ron Taylor. "To think of all the great American heroes who had been there before us . . . and there we were. It was just intoxicating."

One of the most telling facts concerning the Mets' popularity in 1969 was the frequency with which they were written about in the *New York Times*. The *Times*, which ran 352 stories about man landing on the moon, printed 367 stories about the Mets.

Perhaps never before in baseball history was a team as popular with all of America as the 1969 Mets. They struck a common chord in all our hearts. They were not a powerhouse led by superstars, as are most championship teams. Rather, they were a group of young men, who, with a few exceptions, were of mostly average abilities. Yet each did his part, each performed to the very limits of his talent, and sometimes beyond. They believed in themselves when no one else did, and together they became World Champions.

Like the Brooklyn Dodgers of the Fifties, the '69 Mets were the team of the common man. A team of youngsters and veterans, of black and white, of city boys and farm kids, of men from all sections of the nation who came together as one to give us all a shining moment of victory and hope at the end of a decade of social unrest that had confused and angered a nation.

Unselfish, determined, confident, courageous, skilled— are all words that describe the 1969 Mets. They are also words that describe Gil Hodges. Indeed, this team was an extension of Gil Hodges as a man and as an athlete. As the Mets brought America to its feet, Gil Hodges remained in the background, letting the players have their moment in the sun. That was his style. But the players themselves knew in their hearts and minds that it was Gil Hodges who had led them to the summit. It was he who had given them memories that would endure a lifetime. It was he who had made them better ball players, and, more importantly, better human beings.

"They say that a manager only wins a few ball games here and there over the course of a season," says Joe Pignatano, "but Gil Hodges won the 1969 World Championship. All the players know that. He did it with his mind. He had such a fine baseball mind. And you know, whenever the members of that '69 team get together, Gil is always the topic of the day, what he did for them. To me, Gil Hodges was the greatest man I ever knew."

"You will never know," reflects Rube Walker, "how big a role Gil played in the lives of his players, not just as ballplayers, but as men, even after he was gone. He was well respected and well loved. The kids who played for him give him a lot of credit for so many things in their lives. They have said this to me many, many times. You know, it's not the kind of thing you go out and talk to everybody about, but they all loved him very much and appreciate what he did for them as players and as men."

...l finished his playing career as a New York Met in 1963.

Gil took over as the skipper of the Washington Senators in early 1963. Over his ne
five years at the helm, the Senators moved up four places in the standings.

1968 Gil returned home again to New York to manage the Mets. He led them to their best season ever, despite suffering a heart attack in August.

Above: Met skipper Gil Hodges and Director of Player Development Whitey Herzog in the spring of 1968.

Spring training, 1969. Gil had high hopes for his young club.

il Hodges stands at attention during the National Anthem prior to Game Three of
e 1969 World Series.

ctober 16th, 1969...The New York Mets are World Champions. Third baseman Ed
narles jumps for joy as pitcher Jerry Koosman and catcher Jerry Grote embrace on
e mound.

Original Mets manager Casey Stengel hugs Gil Hodges in the clubhouse celebration following the Mets World Series victory in 1969.

PART FOUR

The Last Inning

FOUR

. . . and suddenly he's gone

In 1970 and 1971 Gil Hodges managed the Mets to third place finishes. In each season the Mets fought for the division title until late in the year. They were contenders. With the start of each season the Mets had a legitimate shot at winning the pennant. Gil Hodges had taken the team and made it into one of the best in baseball. He did it not with a squad abundant in talent, but with managerial skill and the ability to get the best from his men.

But if the pressure is enormous on the skipper of a losing or average club, it is tenfold that on the manager of a winner. If the club is a losing or average one, the manager's job is to improve its performance. If he does so, then the season is deemed a success. But with a contending team, the manager is expected to do not less than win the pennant. Suddenly every game on the schedule is an important one. In a close pennant fight, a win or loss in April can make a major difference during the September stretch drive. As the season progresses and the race gets tighter, the pressure intensifies. Especially in the media capital that is New York City. The pressure clamps down on a man. Every move he makes is scrutinized. The dog days of August and September are the worst, when the physical and mental wear and tear of a pressure-filled season lie heavy on a manager. And there is no relief, no escape. With each passing day the pressure builds. Every inning of every game, every pitch thrown, every swing of the bat, every decision a manager makes can mean the difference between becoming a champion or an also-ran.

Gil Hodges never wavered under this strain. At least it didn't show on the outside. As always he kept everything inside him, battling the stress and fatigue from within. He did, however, start smoking again, and smoking heavily.

In early March of 1972 the Mets reported to spring training to prepare for another run at the National League pennant. But on April 1, a week before the season was to begin, the Players Union called the first strike in its history and all baseball operations came to a halt. The Mets were in West Palm Beach, Florida, at the time. The next day, Easter Sunday, Gil Hodges decided to play some golf with coaches Rube Walker, Joe Pignatano and Eddie Yost. They played 27 holes in the humid Florida heat.

"Gilly, what time are we meeting for dinner?" Pignatano asked the manager as they headed off the gold course.

"About 7:30." replied Gil.

A split second later a massive coronary struck Hodges and he collapsed to the pavement. His head hit the ground with a sickening thud. It was 5:10 pm.

Pignatano rushed to his fallen friend's side. Sobbing, he pounded on Gil's chest and slapped his face, looking for some sign of life. Hodges was rushed to Good Samaritan Hospital and admitted to the emergency room at 5:25. He was examined by Dr. James Smith and cardiologist William Donovan. Dr. Donovan did an electrocardiogram that showed "complete heart arrest." At 5:45 on April 2, 1972, just two days short of his 48th birthday, Gil Hodges was pronounced dead.

News of Gil's death shocked and saddened all who knew him, as well as baseball fans across the nation.

"It's a personal loss to me," said Casey Stengel from his home in California. "He was a strong man. He had a strong character underneath a soft exterior. He had a terrific respect for standing up for the rights of others. It's just a sad thing to

see something like this happen. It's sad because he did everything right in his life and suddenly he's gone.'

"He was a great man on the field and off it," said Water
Alston. "It was guys like Hodges, Reese and Campanella who
made it easy for me as a rookie manager with the Dodgers.
All I can say is that there was never a finer man in baseball
than this gentleman. Baseball has lost a great man."

"It was a great shock to me," Leo Durocher said. "He was
a fine man. A good man. A credit to the game on and off the
field. I feel a tremendous loss. I know it will be a great loss to
the city of New York and to the game of baseball."

"The sudden death of Gil Hodges is a deep shock to all
New Yorkers," said Mayor John Lindsay. "As a star of the
immortal Brooklyn Dodgers and as the distinguished manager of the New York Mets, he earned not only the respect
and admiration, but to a greater degree, the friendship of all
baseball fans in New York and the nation. His intense dedication to his work, his enthusiastic spirit and his outstanding
leadership ability will stand as a lesson for all of us."

News of the players' strike faded into the background as
baseball mourned the loss of one of its greatest men. Had it
not been for the strike, the Mets' season would have opened
in Pittsburgh on April 7, but the Pirates would have been the
only team on the field. The Met players were prepared to
forfeit the game out of love and respect for their fallen
leader. "I don't know how they expect to play," said Tom
Seaver the day before the Pirates officially canceled the
game; "all the players will be here [in New York] at the
funeral."

"I wouldn't think of playing that day," said Tommie Agee.
"Gil helped me when I needed him. In his first year, and
mine, I had a terrible time. I went 35 at-bats without a hit. He
stuck with me. I was 0-for-2 *months* and he played me. I
should have been in the minors. But he had gone through it.
He knew how I felt. He always said, 'How do you feel? . . .
Hang in there . . . how's the family?' "

"Even if there weren't any strike, opening day wouldn't mean anything now," said Bud Harrelson through tear-swollen eyes.

At 10:40 am on April 4, Gil Hodges' birthday, a charter flight carrying 37 Yankee players, coaches and front office people took off from Fort Lauderdale. A short time later the plane landed in West Palm Beach to pick up 18 people from the Mets organization and the body of Gil Hodges.

When the plane touched down in West Palm beach, former Met Ron Swoboda was waiting there. "When all the Mets were aboard," wrote Phil Pepe of the *New York Daily News*, "a hearse drove up to the luggage pit and a solitary figure walked slowly to watch the casket being placed in the pit. His eyes misty, Ron Swoboda seemed to be saying farewell to his former manger.

"It is no secret that Ron Swoboda and Gil Hodges did not exactly hit it off, that Swoboda had been critical of the manager's handling of the player, and that their parting exactly one year ago was not an amicable one.

"But Ron Swoboda is not a vindictive man and now he was moved to pay his last respects in his own way and you had to know that Gil Hodges, compassionate man that he was, would have respected him for it. And you had to know, too, that if Ron Swoboda was silently apologizing for things he said, Gil Hodges accepted the apology. . . .

"The trip home from Florida, in most years, is a joyful one. . . . This is the time of year when baseball teams and baseball players are charged up with the excitement of a new season. This is the time of year when an airplane trip from Florida to New York signals a new beginning. This trip was different. It was not a beginning; it was an end."

On April 5, the day before his funeral, Gil Hodges lay in state at Our Lady of Help Roman Catholic Church in Brooklyn. When the casket arrived at 10 am for an 11 am mass, over 2,500 people were lined up outside, 15 abreast. The doors opened to the public at 1 pm ånd when they closed at 10:00 that night more than 36,000 people had come to pay their last respects. In the two hours of viewing before the funeral the next day, thousands more came to say farewell to this much loved and admired man.

He was buried on April 6, 1972, in Holy Cross Cemetery in Brooklyn. The Mets were there. Many of his Brooklyn Dodger teammates were there. Important and influential people from all walks of life were there. And although it was a private service, over 1,500 people stood on the fringes. They stood quietly, saying good-bye to a hero, a friend, but above all, a fine human being.

*   *   *

I REMEMBER EASTER DAY Of 1972 VERY CLEARLY. I HAD gone to church with my mother and kid brother early that morning, and had spent most of the rest of the day gorging myself on the food my mother and aunts made for the holiday. I spent a large part of the day flipping through TV channels catching bits and pieces of the various religious epics that are always aired on Easter Sunday.

At around six o'clock, just as the news came on, I was dozing on the couch in our living room. A number of my relatives were in the house, and the adults were in the kitchen drinking coffee and eating cake. My younger cousins were outside playing. I was the oldest cousin at 16, and if I felt I was too old to play with the kids, I was also too young to sit with the adults. My alternative was to sleep on the couch.

In my drowsiness I heard the TV newscaster mention Gil Hodges' name. I remember thinking that maybe he was quoting Gil on the players' strike. Then I heard the words, "The beloved Mets manager was two days shy of his 48th birthday."

I thought maybe I was dreaming or had heard the anchorman wrong. But in my heart I knew Gil Hodges was dead. I didn't want to wake up because in my sleepiness I thought maybe the whole thing was a bad dream and that if I slept for a while it would all go away.

I forced myself to sit up on the couch and look at the television. I saw the newscaster seated at his desk with a picture of Gil Hodges superimposed over his left shoulder. It was a picture I recognized from the 1971 yearbook. The announcer spoke of a massive heart attack that had taken Gil's life on a golf course in West Palm Beach, Florida. I got up from the couch and walked into the kitchen.

My father must have known something was wrong from the look on my face.

"What's the matter?" he asked.

"Gil Hodges is dead."

All the adults at the table turned to me. "What?" my father said.

"Gil Hodges is dead, Dad. He had a heart attack. I just heard it on the news."

My father and my uncles got up from the table and walked into the living room. By now the newscaster had gone on to the next story, so my father switched channels. On another network I saw the same image I had seen just moments before—an announcer with a picture of Gil superimposed over his left shoulder.

My father, my uncles and I stood in silence as we listened to the details of Gil's death.

Looking back at it now, I realize that my father and my uncles lost a piece of their youth with Gil's death. All had been die-hard Brooklyn Dodger fans as children and as young men. There wasn't a family gathering when they didn't, at some point, talk about the good old days at Ebbets Field. Now they had lost one of the heroes of their youth. I'm sure each of them felt a twinge, and I'm sure each was sobered by the realization of how many years had passed since the summers of their boyhoods.

My father and my uncles spent most of the rest of the evening quietly reminiscing about the Dodgers; about Robinson, Reese, Snider, Campanella, Roe and Gil Hodges. For once I was allowed to sit with the adults. For once there was common ground. Gil Hodges had been one of their heroes, but he had also been mine. I didn't say anything; I just sat and listened to the tales of their youthful days spent at Ebbets Field.

That night I went into my closet and pulled out my treasured 1962 Mets yearbook. I turned to the page Gil Hodges had signed. I felt a deep sadness and sense of loss as I stared at his picture. I had always thought I'd get the chance to meet him again. I couldn't believe that it had been 10 years since that rainy day at the Polo Grounds when I'd met him.

I lay down on my bed and closed my eyes. In my mind I could clearly see Gil Hodges standing in front of me. He was smiling and talking and I was just standing there with my mouth hanging open, not believing what was happening to me.

I opened my eyes and smiled as a rush of warmth came over me. I realized how fortunate I was. I had had the opportunity to spend a few moments with my boyhood idol, and he had given me one of the fondest and most cherished memories of my life. I thought of all the kids who never had that chance, or who had it and were disappointed. I had not been disappointed.

Now, whenever I see a picture of Gil Hodges or hear his name mentioned, my mind drifts back over the years to a rainy summer day at the Polo Grounds; to a day when a young boy stood in front of his idol, and for a time all was right with the world.

*   *   *

IN THE END THE TRUE MEASURE OF A MAN IS NOT what he accomplished in his lifetime, but how he touched the lives of other people. In this respect Gil Hodges was truly a great man. He touched the thousands of fans around the nation who loved, respected and admired him, and who thrilled to his achievements as a player and a manager. He touched the people of Brooklyn who, from the day he arrived in the city, adopted him as their own. He touched the thousands of kids who looked up to him as a hero and a role model, and Gil never faltered in the example he set for them.

Together with his Brooklyn Dodger teammates, Gil fought the battle against the injustice and bigotry that faced Jackie Robinson, and together they won. Prejudice, hate and intolerance had no place in Gil's world.

He touched the lives of the men who played under him as a manager, and they give him credit not only for making them better ballplayers, but better human beings as well. And just by being himself, and by being true to what he believed in, he touched every person who ever came in contact with him. Even those who didn't have the privilege of knowing him personally were touched by the man's great dignity, honesty, decency and humility.

And today, almost two decades after his death, his name and spirit are alive everywhere in Brooklyn. Little league diamonds throughout the borough are adorned with signs proclaiming them "Home of Gil Hodges Little League." Businesses and stores all over Brooklyn display placards stating proudly that they are "Sponsors of Gil Hodges Little League." Walk down almost any street in the city and you will see youngsters and adults of all ages wearing a nylon warm-up jacket with the words "Gil Hodges Baseball Club" emblazoned across the back. The bridge that crosses the inlet between Brooklyn and Rockaway is named the Gil Hodges Memorial Bridge. And if you drive east on the Belt Parkway, from Manhattan toward Brooklyn, you will see on your left—amidst the tangle of roads, subway tracks, buildings and all the other trappings of an urban setting—a patch of green. It is a little league ball park. And high above the park is a large orange and blue sign that looms over the highway and can be seen from anywhere in the area. The sign reads: GIL HODGES STADIUM. Looking at it, you have to know that Gil was far prouder of having a little league park named after him than he would have been had a big league stadium been named in his honor.

For his own part, Gil Hodges would have wished to be remembered simply as a family man, a man dedicated to his wife, his children, his community and his God. To Gil Hodges, these were the most important things in the world. And yes, he will be remembered as this, and as a genuine hero as well.

Brooklyn's Bishop Francis Mugavaro often pointed to Gil's abiding love for country, family and truth as an example for us all. It was an example that did not die with the man.

And in singling out one athlete, one man, to symbolize the integrity, character, courage, decency, dignity, honesty, humility and sportsmanship of an entire city and its people, Brooklyn could have found no better man than Gil Hodges.

As a player, a manager and a man, few players in baseball history were as beloved as number 14, Gil Hodges.

Gil (*right*) and teammate, pitcher Sal Maglie, celebrate a Dodger victory in 1956.

Left to right: Pee Wee Reese, Gil Hodges and Carl Erskine in 1957, the Dodgers last season in Brooklyn.

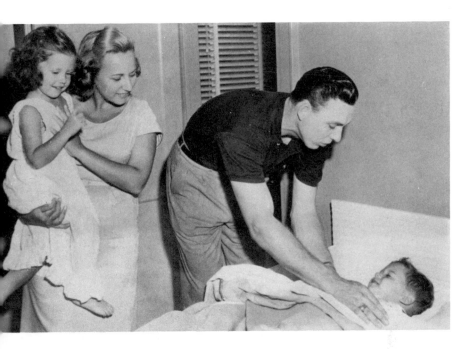

o Gil, the family was the most important thing. Here he tucks in Gil, Jr. while wife oan and daughter Irene look on.

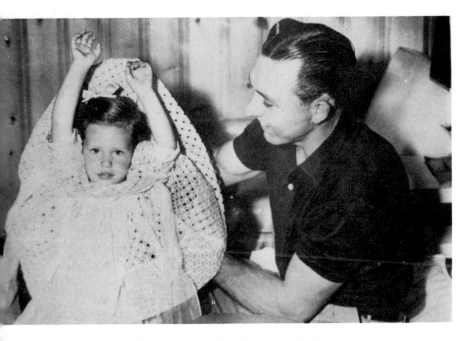

il and daughter Irene at home in Brooklyn in the early 1950s.

Gil at Ebbets Field in 1953. He hit 31 home runs that season to help lead the Dodge to their fourth pennant in seven years.

Gil in spring training of 1962 with the New York Mets. Seven years later as their manager, he would lead them to the top of the baseball world.

Gil signs an autograph for a young fan in early March of 1972. A month later he w
dead of a massive heart attack.

PART FIVE

Remembering Gil

FIVE

*If you had a son, it would be a great thing
to have him grow up just like Gil Hodges*

CARL ERSKINE

Pitcher, Brooklyn & L.A. Dodger Teammate, 1948–1959

There were a number of leaders on the club, Pee Wee, Jackie, and, of course, Gil. Each of them was a leader in his own way. Gil was a very quiet and private person, but everybody on the club looked up to him because of his dedication and his strength and character.

Gil was always true to what be believed in as a player, a man and a parent. There was absolutely no phoniness about him. You knew that what he believed in ran very deep. He was committed to his family and his Catholic faith.

I remember that Gil would never argue on a pitch, even if it was an obviously bad call. He would just accept it and wait for the next pitch. Even the players would get on Gil about that. I mean, seriously get on him. They'd say, "Gil, you have to protect yourself up there. That umpire is taking the bat out of your hands." But Gil felt, it was over, what could he change? He'd go up and take care of it in the next at-bat.

I'll tell you something that will give you a real illustration of the kind of man he was. It was in Chicago and Tom Gorman, as I recall, was the umpire, and he called Gil out on a real bad low strike. Gil came back to the bench, put his bat in the rack, quietly laid down his helmet and quietly sat

135

down. The next time up he got called out again on an obviously bad pitch. He did the same thing when he got back to the bench, only this time the players really got on him. Our bench—Robinson, Snider and those guys—are saying, "Gil, you have to show some initiative up there. Let that umpire know you're there. He's killing you with those bad calls."

Well, they kept getting on Gil and really letting him have it. Finally Gil, kind of disgusted with the whole thing, looks up and says, "Okay, okay, next time up there I'm not even going to ask him how his wife and kids are."

I don't ever remember Gil showing any great emotion for any situation. He pretty much stayed on an even keel. I'm sure a lot of emotions were going on underneath, but we never saw it. I'm sure he enjoyed the high points we had, and I'm sure he felt the agony of the losing, too. When he went 0-for-21 in the 1952 World Series he must have agonized beyond anyone's imagination, but you never saw it on the outside. See, Gil had a side to him that probably only those people really close to him knew.

At first base Gil was the best I ever saw. He had great footwork and great range. And boy, did he have good hands. Just tremendous in size, but soft. He never dropped anything that was near him. He was so smooth he made difficult plays look easy. Like throwing to the pitcher covering the bag. He was a master at it. The throw was always perfect, even if his momentum in catching the ball was carrying him toward second.

He was a very stabilizing and calming presence in the infield. He was great at reading strategies and stealing signs. The best on the team at it. He would have signs stolen and he would know what the other team was going to do, and he'd come in and tell the pitcher in certain situations. It was a great help. If you were in a tough situation, Gil would come over and say a few words and it really made you calm down and concentrate. He had a real knack for that.

It was a surprise to me when Gil became a manager. Gil knew the game as well as anybody, but it was a question of whether or not he had the right kind of personality. We always felt that Campanella would have made a great manager, and, of course, Pee Wee, but it really surprised me when Gil was the one who ended up becoming a manager. I think, though, we saw that quiet strength come through, and he certainly demonstrated his ability to handle men. I've talked to some of the players he managed, and from what I understand, he was pretty tough.

When Gil died we were devastated. We knew he was a heavy smoker, and the pressure of managing, especially in New York, must have been enormous. We also knew that all these emotions we never saw were taking place inside him and taking their toll. It was a terrible tragedy. He was such a good man. A strong man. I think in his own quiet way he had an effect on all of us. I'm glad I had the opportunity to know him. I'm a better person for it. I think everybody who knew Gil Hodges is a better person for having known him.

CLEM LABINE

Pitcher, Brooklyn Dodger Teammate, 1950–1960

Gil Hodges was the quiet man. A great strength. A great physical being as far as stature and athletic build were concerned. He was able to quell fights caused by someone else whether on the field or in the clubhouse. He had a unique ability to have people really like and respect him by being such a strong, quiet man.

He demanded respect from everyone just by his presence. Quiet people can do that sometimes if they have that strength of character, which Gilly did. There wasn't anything phony about Gil either on the field or off. You had to respect him for what he was and what he believed in. He was deeply religious and dedicated to his family. To Gil, that was the most important thing, his family.

Gil was always the same no matter if we were winning or losing, whether he was hitting or not, he was always consistent. I'd have to say he was a real stabilizing force on the team, especially when you consider the colorful characters we had on that club.

I remember one time, though, when Gil kind of broke out of his mold. This was probably in the mid-Fifties and we happened to be in Pittsburgh. Pittsburgh was a real quiet town for us. We stayed in a hotel up on Schenley Hill right near the ball park, and there wasn't much activity. The most activity was the evening meal, and then we went to play the ball game that night.

At that time Gilly had been in just a horrendous slump, and this particular day he went 0-for-4 again. So that night he gathered a bunch of us when we came into the hotel. They had this little bar there and he got about 12 of us, including Jackie Robinson, who didn't even drink, and we went into the bar and he told the bartender to lock the door. Now Gilly wasn't a drinker, but on this night he walked up to the bar, pounded on it and said, "The drinks are on me and we're not leaving until we get pie-eyed." That was so out of character for Gil we just couldn't believe it, then we all started to laugh. Well, we got pie-eyed and the next day Gilly went 2-for-4.

To tell you the truth, I was really surprised when Gilly became a manager. If I had to pick anyone on our club and put him into what I consider a managerial mold, I would have never even considered Gilly. He had that quiet frustration about him. With Gil almost everything was internal. I guess him dying at such a young age might prove the stress he was always under that none of us really realized.

His death was a very sobering and shocking thing when you consider the physical attributes he had. The only thing I can say was that Gil always kept everything inside and he was a heavy smoker. Of all of us, it was really shocking that Gilly was the first to die.

PEE WEE REESE

Shortstop, Brooklyn & L.A. Dodger Teammate, 1947–1958

Gil Hodges was class. That's how I would describe Gil. He was just one of the best people I ever knew in baseball, or anywhere else.

When Gil first came up he was very shy, but over time, in his own way, he became a leader. Everybody had a great deal of respect for Gil. Of all the ballplayers I've ever met, here was a guy you knew would never do anything wrong. I don't care where he was or what he was doing, he was always going to be Gil Hodges husband of Joan Hodges and that's that.

Having Gil as a first baseman all those years was a great thing for a shortstop. If I threw the ball in the dirt he'd save me. But I used to kid him a lot. Say I got to a ball deep in the hole to my right and made a throw Gil couldn't handle, which was rare, I'd say, "Jeez Gil, I have to catch those short-hops all day out there at shortstop, and then I throw you one short-hop, you see it all the way across the infield and you still can't come up with it, and *I* get the error." Then Gil would say, "Pee Wee, get the damn ball up."

He had great hands. They were so large, and boy, with those hands he could throw some kind of knuckleball. I used to warm up with him, but finally I had to quit. He would love to throw you a knuckleball when you were warming up, and it would break so severe that it would miss your glove and hit you in the chest. And I'd say, "Gil, stop throwing those damn things." He'd just stand there and laugh.

He was a very sweet individual, but you get him in a game and he was a great competitor. He would never give any outward sign that he was frustrated or having a bad time at the plate. He'd always walk into the clubhouse with that grin on his face. With Gil, you never knew whether he was hitting .500 or hadn't had a hit in 10 games. He was always the same.

I think everyone on the Dodgers was surprised when Gil became a manager. I guess everybody thought I was the one who would become a manager, but I didn't want it. Too much pressure. It takes too much out of you. With Gil, he knew baseball and he could handle men, but I never thought Gil had the right personality to be a big league manager. But hell, he became a great manager. You don't win the pennant and the World Series unless you know what you're doing.

Still, I think the pressure and tension of the job may have had something to do with causing his heart attack.

I was shocked and sickened by Gil's death. Even though I have often said the pressures of the job may have contributed to his death, I never thought it would happen. . . . I just never thought it would.

I saw him in Florida just a few days before he died. I remember I always used to kid him and say, "You big so-and-so, one of these days you're just going to fall apart." Gil would laugh and say, "Don't say that, Pee Wee." But I never thought it could happen. I just couldn't picture it. He was such a strong and such a good person. I can't even describe to you how sickened I was when he died. I guess one of the nicest things I can say about Gil is this. If you had a son, it would be a great thing to have him grow up to be just like Gil Hodges. I know that's a cliché but with Gil it's true. He was just a helluva man. I had such a warm feeling about him. Everybody admired and respected Gil because of the kind of man he was. He was the type of guy you would want for a friend or a son or a father or anything you can name. He would be my ideal man.

ROY CAMPANELLA

Catcher, Brooklyn Dodger Teammate, 1948–1957

I thought Gil was just a wonderful person with a tremendous outlook on life. He was just a tremendous all-around ballplayer and a fine human being.

He was never booed anyplace. That's rare. But the fans just knew Gil. They knew what kind of man he was, so they never booed him. You'd never see Gil get thrown out of a ball game or argue with an umpire. Never. He was a leader on our team. Everybody respected Gil and looked up to him.

I remember when I joined the Dodgers in 1948, Gil was the third-string catcher. I recall that one day Leo Durocher called the both of us into his office and told Gil he was going to play first base and I would be the catcher. He wanted both our bats in the lineup. Gil, of course, went on to become the best first baseman in the league. In fact, he was the best I ever saw.

I'd have to say I was surprised when Gil took up managing. He really didn't seem like the type to be a manager. I remember we used to tease him in the clubhouse all the time because he would never argue with an umpire. But he turned out to be a tremendous manager. Outstanding.

When I got the news that he had had a heart attack on the golf course and died, I just couldn't believe it. He was the picture of health. When you talk about a guy that was in great shape, so big and strong, you're talking about Gil. His death was just so hard to accept. He was just a great human being whom everybody respected. Everybody liked Gil Hodges.

You know, looking at it now you see that all the things that have happened to the men on our team are, I think, just a part of life. People always say, "Look at all those things that have happened to those fellows on the Brooklyn Dodgers." But you know, the same things have happened to millions of other people, with the exception that they weren't Brooklyn Dodgers. I mean, how many people have heart attacks and drop dead? Millions do. Not just Gil Hodges. Not just Jackie Robinson. But how many Jackie Robinsons were there? Just one. How many Gil Hodgeses were there? Just one.

Gil Hodges was a Hall-of-Fame man all the way. He belongs there. It's tough to get in, but he belongs. I'll tell you, though, Gil Hodges is in my Hall of Fame.

PREACHER ROE

Pitcher, Brooklyn Dodger Teammate, 1948–1954

I thought Gil Hodges was the tops. In the last few years I've tried to pattern myself after Gil. You know, being more reserved and quiet. That's the kind of man he was, the kind of guy you would want to be like.

Gil was just so consistent. If something good happened for us he would always show a little emotion. You know, he'd give you a big smile and a pat on the back, but he was never over-exuberant.

Whatever Gil did he was always the same. I think that's part of the reason why he was never booed. See, I think a lot of times most players bring the boos on themselves. In other words, if a man looks bad, then shows too much reaction to what he's done, he looks twice as bad. Gil was never like that. He was always consistent. He never showed dislike for anybody, not even the umpires, so why should anybody dislike him? Everybody just respected him.

Gil was great at first base. When you were pitching it was good to know he was out there. Not just because of his defense, but because of his knowledge, too. He really knew baseball and could always tell what the other team was going to do. That was a real help to a pitcher. Also, in a tight situation he would come to the mound and calm you down. Just knowing he was out there behind you made you feel better. Now, that's the kind of thing you don't see in the record book, but there were a lot of things Gil did like that.

I never thought Gil would be a manager. He was just so good-natured and mild-mannered and easygoing. But he proved himself, didn't he? Winning the World Series and all.

When Gil died I was so upset I didn't know what to think. I mean, I could see where a man like Jackie Robinson might have a heart attack because he was so hyper and active and controversial. But not Gil. You just thought with Gil that here was a man who was going to live forever.

CARL FURILLO

Outfielder, Brooklyn & L.A. Dodger Teammate,
1947–1960

I was Gil's roommate for over 10 years on the Dodgers, and it was one of the greatest things that ever happened to me in baseball. Gil was just a big leaguer in every way; in the way he was on and off the field, in the way he dealt with other people. I don't know of any other man I ever knew whom I respected more than Gil. He was the kind of guy you would want to be like, to model yourself after.

Gil was always the same no matter how the team was doing or how he was doing. He was a real leader on our club and he led by example. He never had a whole lot to say, so when he did say something you listened.

I knew Gil pretty good because I roomed with him all those years, and I never thought he was the type to become a manager. He was so quiet and he always kept everything inside, so it was hard to picture him running a ball club. But he did a helluva job, didn't he? Winning the world championship.

I'm sure the pressure of managing a ball club, especially in New York, got to Gil. But he kept it all inside like he always did and I guess that was one of the reasons for the heart attack that killed him. I was so shocked by his death, so sad. I never had a better friend than Gil Hodges. He was a man you could always count on. I'll never forget him, and a day doesn't go by when I don't think of him.

DUKE SNIDER

Outfielder, Brooklyn & L.A. Dodger Teammate,
1947–1961

Gil and I knew each other in 1947 before I got sent down to St. Paul. We shared a room in a home on Bedford Avenue not far from the ball park. I got to know Gil as a very serious and dedicated man as far as life and baseball were concerned.

Gil was a great student of the game of baseball. He knew the game exceptionally well. He taught himself how to perform in key situations. He really analyzed everything. In his own way Gil was a tremendous leader. He led by example. He was very quiet but he could needle a guy pretty good when he wanted to. He had that dry wit and dry sense of humor about him.

He was a very steady person and a great teammate. He was the type of guy you just couldn't dislike. I don't think there was anybody on the team that didn't care for him. We all had a lot of respect for him, and we would marvel at the way he could perform.

I guess I knew Gil a little different than some of the other guys, and I wasn't surprised when he became a manager. He was a leader, no question about that. He was an ex-Marine and he learned a lot in the Marine Corp about adapting himself to any situation. I was rooming with him with the Mets in 1963 when he left to manage the Washington club and I knew he would do a good job. He studied the game so thoroughly and was such a student of the game that there was no question in my mind he would make a good manager.

It was a very, very sad day when Gil died. I heard about it on the radio and I felt like I had lost someone in my family. I didn't go to Gil's funeral, or Jackie's either. I'm the type of person who prefers to remember a person the way they were. That's how I want to remember Gil.

DON DRYSDALE

Pitcher, Brooklyn & L.A. Dodger Teammate, 1956–1961

I roomed with Gil from the time I came up in 1956 until he went over to the Mets in 1962. It was the greatest thing that ever happened to me in the game of baseball. He was like a big brother, a second father. He taught me everything I know about being a big leaguer. I remember I couldn't wait to get out on the road just so I could be with him.

He was a great all-around ball player and probably the best first baseman I ever saw. I remember in Brooklyn one day he made two errors, which was very rare for him. The errors happened because the two of us couldn't get together on ground balls to first where I was supposed to cover the bag. But Gil was very calm about the whole thing. That's the way he was. He said, "Roomie, we have to work on this," and that was it. That's the way he talked. And, of course, we worked it out.

I guess I knew Gil better than most because I roomed with him all those years. On the outside he was always calm, at least in public and on the field, but he was human. He'd get mad sometimes. Let's set the record straight. When we were alone he'd get hot and swear. But that alone will tell you he kept a lot inside.

Funny thing, in all the time we spent together he never talked about his time in the Marines. One of his nicknames was "Marine," but he never talked about being in the service. And you wouldn't dare ask him about his time over there. It's just a question you didn't ask Gil Hodges out of respect for him. Every now and then on the road, when we were eating dinner, someone would come up to him and say, "Hi, I'm so-and-so and I was in the Marines." And Gil would say, "How are you? How's your family?" but he would never talk about the war or what he did over there. I wish I would have tracked it down more with some of the people who were over there with Gil, because Gil himself would never talk about it.

It didn't surprise me at all when Gil became a manager. I knew he would be a good manager and I knew the kind of respect he would command from his players. I would say that Gil took a chapter from the Walter Alston way of managing. Alston was the same way. He wouldn't bother a flea, but he expected you to give your best all the time and have your mind on the ball game. We'd have a meeting every once and a while and Alston would chew out everybody's ass. It didn't matter who you were or how long you'd been playing. And that would be it for another month or so. But Alston made sure you knew how he felt. Gil was the same way.

When I was broadcasting I'd see Gil and Rube Walker and Joe Pignatano and I'd always ask Rube or Piggy, "How's my roomie doing?'' And they'd say, "All right, but he's about ready for another goddam explosion. These sons of bitches can't play worth a damn." Then I'd talk to Gil and I'd see that he was very disturbed by the lack of fundamentals in his players. When we played for the Dodgers we were taught very sound fundamental baseball. That's the way it was in the Dodger organization, and it was something Gil tried very hard to instill in his players. Sometimes it was very tough for him to comprehend how his players hadn't had the schooling in the fundamentals that we had with the Dodgers.

I can't describe to you my feelings when Gil died. It hurt deeply. Here was a man I looked up to, a man I respected and loved. The man who taught me how to be a big leaguer. He touched my life in so many ways. . . . I look at it as a privilege, a blessing, that I knew Gil as well as I did . . . that he considered me his friend.

You know, I talk baseball with people all the time, and whenever Gil's name comes up in a conversation everyone gets quiet and listens closely. It's an amazing thing to see. The man was so loved and so respected. When that happens I always have to smile . . . and I think about my roomie, and I'm grateful to have had the privilege of knowing him, and that he was a part of my life.

FRANK HOWARD

Outfielder, L.A. Dodger Teammate, 1958–1961
Played Under Hodges 1965–1967, Washington Senators

I have three sons of my own, and if any one of them, or all three, can grow up to be just half the man Gil Hodges was, my wife and I will be lighting candles in church for the rest of our lives. The point being, when you talk about a sense of respect, of decency, of honor and fairness; when you talk about class and style, you're talking about Gil Hodges.

He was a very dapper man, very orderly and disciplined. I think he represents everything that America has tried to teach its young men in growing up and reaching manhood. He projected everything we look for in our own kids; and things we look for in ourselves, too. But he would be a tough guy to emulate because he had so many outstanding qualities.

I played with him for four years as a young man, and he and Pee Wee Reese, Duke Snider, Carl Erskine were great people to break in under, because they taught you how to be a big leaguer. They took the young kids out to dinner and tried to make you feel an important part of the ball club, and things like that. They took great pride in the organization they played for and they wanted the young players who came along to feel that same pride.

Gil was like that with the young players. A real leader. He didn't lead by being an extrovert; he led by example. He had that quiet dignity and that great class and style, and you learned from just being around him. He also had a very dry wit and a great sense of humor.

I know that when I had conversations with him when I was a young player it really helped me a lot. He took me under his wing. You see, being a big leaguer isn't just a measure of ability, it is a way of conducting yourself, too. Gil stressed that. Always be clean shaven, always have your hair combed, always dress well, because that was the big league way of doing things. He felt that because you are a major league ballplayer, a lot of people, especially kids, look to you as a role model and you had a responsibility to set a good example. He felt very strongly about that.

When I played for Gil on the Senators I was at a very crucial point in my career. I had just gotten traded from the Dodgers and I really had my doubts about being an everyday player. I had been platooned in Los Angeles and after a while you begin to wonder, can I do it? Can I play every day? But Gil gave me the opportunity to play on a regular basis and he really worked with me. He devoted a lot of time, energy and patience. I've had some great managers, but Gil was the best for me. He leveled with me and was completely objective, fair and honest. He said, "Frank, you're at the stage in your career where you better start *thinking* about baseball. You better start thinking about what that guy is doing 60 feet away. You better start thinking about what base to throw to in any situation."

Gil stressed two major things—fundamentals and giving your best all the time. If you didn't do that you were in trouble. He didn't yell or anything, but he was a tough guy and he could accomplish more with a cold stare of those steely blue eyes, and you got the message in a hurry. He didn't have to raise his voice. But when he did you knew that he was really mad and you better straighten up or you wouldn't be part of his team much longer.

If you made a mistake he would let you know in no uncertain terms how he felt, but he'd do it in private. He'd never embarrass you, but he'd make sure you never made the same mistake again. That was his style. That's not to say it was the only way, but it worked for Gil. Everything the man did he did with a purpose, and always with a sense of style and dignity.

His door was always open if you needed to talk to him. He was a very compassionate and understanding man. He would listen. If a guy was having problems or struggling, Gil would get out there early to give him extra work, or have a bull session with him to reassure the guy and build up his confidence.

He was the type of guy who remained poised 99 percent of the time. He had complete control of his emotions. I think there are a lot of people who think he would have been better off if he could have found a release for his frustration and anger. But who knows? When you say that you are just speculating. He'd blow his stack once or twice a year and really let you have an earful, but who knows if that was enough?

Managing in the big leagues is a demanding job, but it seemed to me he had the ability to handle the pressure. He could take the heat. Still, I think every guy needs a release, and Gil had very few outlets for that. Whether or not it would have prolonged his life, who's to say?

I think it's just a question of time before Gil goes into the Hall of Fame. There's no question that he belongs there. Gil Hodges is a Hall of Famer plain and simple. I mean, Gil and I had a couple of times when we didn't see eye-to-eye, but you know, as you get older and smarter you say, "Damn, he was right and I was wrong."

I don't think he ever steered a guy in the wrong direction. I really believe that. He helped you grow up and be a man. He taught you not only baseball, but he instructed you in life, too. He was, I think, a great human being; not infallible—none of us are—but he had as many good qualities as you'll find in any person.

What happened to Gil was really tragic and heartbreaking. Here's a guy that should have lived to be 100, and who knows what he would have accomplished and how many more lives he would have touched had he lived a full life? But he was a great human being, and anybody who had the good fortune to know him is a better person because of it. He was a man who was genuinely loved, not only in New York, but all across America.

JERRY KOOSMAN

Pitcher, Played Under Hodges
1968–1971, New York Mets

To me, Gil Hodges was the best manager I've ever seen because he had the talent of knowing not just your physical capabilities, but your mental capabilities as well. When he saw a situation arise that he knew certain players couldn't handle, either mentally or physically, he got them out of there. Because of this he made us all look good. He never let any of us get a big head no matter how good we were doing. He always instilled a lot of confidence in us, and pride too.

He used all 25 guys to win the championship in 1969. Nobody got rusty.

Say somebody had a bad game or made a bad play; well if that situation came up again he'd bring that guy back—a relief pitcher, a pinch hitter, whatever—this way the guy got his confidence back. It kept us all sharp. He just didn't put you out to pasture if you had a bad game.

Gil was strict but he was fair, and he didn't lose his temper much; but boy when he did, you better listen. He made the rules and you had to obey them. There was no arguing about that. If you broke a rule it didn't matter if you'd won six games in a row or lost six in a row, if you were a veteran or not, you got fined. He treated everybody the same. Nobody on the club was more important than anybody else.

Now, maybe some of the veteran players didn't like Gil's system all that much, but they respected him for it; and us younger players, we never knew any other way.

Gil instilled a feeling of pride in us. He taught us to be big leaguers on the field and off. It was a standing rule with Gil that his team had to wear jackets and ties on the road. It doesn't seem like much, but when people saw us they'd say, "There is a good-looking group of young men." See, Gil's ways made us gentlemen. We always had pride in ourselves. And that's something that carries over into your life. You always give your best and you always take pride in your self. Because of Gil all of us became better people. I was fortunate to have him as a manager as a young player. He taught me lessons that will stay with me the rest of my life.

BUD HARRELSON

Shortstop, Played Under Hodges
1968–1971, New York Mets

I haven't played for a lot of managers, but as far as I'm concerned, no one could scratch the surface of what Gil Hodges was. He was the best. He could figure people out and he knew how to talk to them.

When we got Gil in 1968 he really didn't know any of the players that well, having been in the American League; so that year he made evaluations. I think he made suggestions to the front office on how the club could be improved and that we needed a little bit more depth. But basically, in 1968, I think he kind of sat back and observed what he had to work with.

Then, in 1969, Gil really went to work. He explained things very simply to us. He told us that we had lost 36 one-run games in '68, and if we'd won those games we would have been tied for first place or been in first place. So he tried to break things down and simplify them.

I remember he said, "If every pitcher on our staff wins one more game than he loses, with 11 pitchers, we're going to finish 11 games over .500." He broke it down like that. I think by doing this it took the pressure off a long season and made it a day-to-day thing.

He was very subtle, very low key. If you did something wrong, he didn't scream "Why did you do that!" Instead he'd ask you very calmly, "Why did you try and steal home with two outs?" I thought about it and said, "Well, maybe I shouldn't have gone." He said, "No," because he was looking for a specific answer. He was trying to make me think a little bit. So I'm beating around the bush, trying to come up with an answer, and finally Gil says, "Who was hitting?" I said, "Boswell." He said, "Boswell's had a hot bat lately; you should have given him a chance to win the game." Obviously there were a number of reasons why I shouldn't have gone, but they were not the ones Gil wanted to hear. He wanted to make a specific point and when he made it he'd say, "Good, that's right; see you tomorrow and have a good night." That was his style. The most important thing was he wanted to make you think, to use your head.

I remember one night in 1969 I came to the ball park and I felt terrible. I think I had a 104-degree temperature or something like that. The trainer apparently told Gil I was sick, so Gil called me into his office. He said, "I'll tell you what; you play tonight and I'll give you tomorrow off." I said, "Fine, I didn't go into the trainer's room to get out of playing; I just wanted to get something to make me feel better." But just because Gil said that to me I felt good because I knew he wanted me in there. Well, I went out that night and got three hits. After the game I went into Gil's office and said, "If I have a 110-degree temperature tomorrow, I'm playing." He just smiled and said, "Okay, you're the boss."

That summer I was in the Army reserve and I had to go to two weeks of training camp in Connecticut, so I was able to play only the home games for those two weeks. It was rough. I'd get up at five in the morning and go to camp until five at night; then I'd come to the ball park and sleep in the trainer's room until game time. Gil was the only person who would come and wake me up. He'd come in and say, "I don't care if you don't get a hit tonight; just go out there and play shortstop. Don't worry about your hitting." By saying this to me he gave me confidence because I knew he wanted me in there. It also made me more relaxed because I wasn't going to get all uptight if I didn't hit the ball so well.

You see, all along he would talk to me, he would coach me, thinking-wise and professional-wise, and by doing subtle things, and by talking to me and getting into my head, he made me a better ballplayer.

I was good defensively and I was a pesky little hitter, but Gil took it farther than that. He taught me a lot. He taught me to look for that fire in players.

Gil really made a difference in my life. He made me a better player and a better person. He was like a father to me.

JERRY GROTE

Catcher, Played Under Hodges
1968–1971, New York Mets

I wasn't set as a ballplayer or a person until Gil Hodges came along. He settled me down and encouraged me to think. I'll never forget the first time I walked into his office in 1968. I asked him about a move he had made, and Gil just about came unglued. He started letting me have it about second-guessing him and that I was never to do that. I said, "Wait a minute, Gil; you've got me wrong here. I'm not second-guessing. You told me that whenever I wanted to know something to come and ask you. I want to know why you did what you did because if the same situation comes up against another ball club, I want to know what you're thinking so I can set the defense."

Well, Gil smiled and explained it to me. From then on we had a great relationship. I went into Gil's office many times. I'd ask him why he did something, or why he thought another manager made a certain move, and we'd talk about it. I learned a lot from him and I became a much better ballplayer.

Gil really helped me with my hitting. He changed my whole stance around in 1968 and it made a world of difference. I was the starting catcher on the National League All-Star team in 1968, and my improved hitting had a lot to do with it. I hit .195 the year before, and by mid-season of 1968 I was hitting in the high .280s. But Gil was like that. If he knew you were really serious about improving a part of your game, he would put in a lot of time with you and work with you. He was dedicated to his players like that. I never knew another manager who would do that.

When Gil came to the club in 1968, the first thing he did was establish who was boss. He made it clear that you didn't cross him. He took a real tough line. In 1968 whenever he called you into his office it was usually for an ass-chewing. But even that shows you what kind of man he was. He wouldn't do it in front of everybody, which a lot of managers do. If Gil wanted to discipline you or let you have it, he did it in the privacy of his office, or maybe he'd talk to you on the field, but never in front of anybody to embarrass you.

I'll never forget the one thing in 1968 that really showed me what kind of guy he was. One day he called me into his office to ask about a throw from the outfield that had gotten away from me. The thing he didn't understand is why I had kept my mask on. He said, "Jerry, don't you think you'd have a better view of the ball if you took your mask off and threw it aside?" I said, "Well, I'll tell you why I kept in on. I've got what I feel is a legitimate reason. I see every pitch that is thrown to me with my mask on, so it's not like it's something new. Hell, a short hop or a good hop is easy to catch. But the one that got away from me was one of those bastard in-between hops. You take a shot at it and either you get it or you don't. Now, if I keep my mask on I'm going to keep my head in there and watch the ball all the way. But if I take if off I might turn my head away, and then I have no chance at all. So I kept it on."

Gil was quiet for a second, then said, "Okay, you answered my question. That's fine." That shows you how fair Gil was.

He stressed two things above all. First, you better be hustling your ass off all the time or you were going to be out of there. Also, Gil stressed fundamentals. Basic fundamentals. He always wanted you thinking out there. If we got out-hit or out-pitched and lost a game, that was one thing. But if we lost because of a mental error, Gil would get on your ass about that.

I don't think any of us realized at the time the kind of effect Gil was having on us as men. But as you get older you realize things, and I know he made me a better individual in a lot of ways. He had an impact on everybody he touched. He got respect and he didn't have to work for it because everybody knew what kind of man he was. He was a great baseball man, and he was a great human being.

TOM SEAVER

Pitcher, Played Under Hodges
1968–1971, New York Mets

During the St. Louis-Boston World Series of 1967, the Mets announced that Gil Hodges would be the new manager.

There's no way to measure the difference that he made. I have to tip my hat to Gil Hodges. He worked as hard in a manager's way as any of us. When we won he was as proud.

It isn't taking anything away from anybody to say that Gil Hodges will have a lot to do with anything accomplished in the future by the fellows who played for him. He was a leader who impressed on us the need for excellence. He didn't expect perfection. That was too much to ask. But he always wanted us to work for perfection and that wasn't too much to ask. His standards were high, and he encouraged me to set mine high too. Some guys were intimidated by him. Then they understood how human and warm he was.

He had his first heart attack in September, 1968, when he was just 44 years old. He worked very hard that winter to be able to manage again in 1969, and it seems right that the day we clinched the Eastern Division Championship was exactly one year later.

He lived his life the only way he could. He limited what he did physically as much as he could. He dieted away the excess weight. But he couldn't protect himself from the stress of winning and losing.

DONN CLENDENON

First Baseman, Played Under Hodges
1969-1971, New York Mets

When I came to the Mets in June of 1969, Gil and I had a long talk and I knew the role he wanted me to play. It was a young team and I was a veteran player, so he wanted me to assume a leadership role, which I did.

Gil was a very strong individual. I think you can rank him as one of the best managers ever. One of the things I liked about Gil was that he would listen. He was always fair about things.

I remember one time he called me into his office and said that he had heard that Agee, Jones and I were out partying until four or five in the morning. I said, "Gil, I respect you because you've helped me a lot at first base, but I don't like being accused of anything. If you want to know if I've been out all night just ask me. Fuck no, I have not and never have. Do you ever see me with Agee or Jones except at the ball park? No. After the game I go my own way."

So Gil called Agee and Jones in and asked them. Agee told him that it wasn't me, it was Willie Davis. I said, "Gil, I'm always in my room. I might be reading. I might have a date in my room. But I learned a long time ago there's nothing out there in the streets for me."

Gil smiled, and that was the end of that. If you were honest and open with him he respected you for it and was fair with you. But you didn't ever lie to him and you didn't argue with him.

One of the things I admired about Gil was the way he handled the kids. See, when you take young minds and make them believe that if they work hard and get in good condition they can't lose, it's amazing what they can do. Gil did that. He was a strong leader and he never wavered. He always believed we could win, and he made us believers too, especially the young players. Because of Gil these kids thought they were great ballplayers. I had tears in my eyes after we won the Series. Here are guys like Garrett, Boswell, Swoboda, who were not what you would call consummate ballplayers, and they're walking around with their chests out; it was just unbelievable. I remember I turned to Joe Pignatano and said, "Piggy, this is just incredible." And it was.

We were a good team, no question. We had some raw talent, we had great pitching, a good defense, and we played smart heads-up baseball, but it was Gil Hodges who molded those young guys into champions.

CLEON JONES

Outfielder, Played Under Hodges 1968–1971, New York Mets

Gil Hodges was the best manager I ever played for. He had an ability to read into an individual and get out what he didn't know he had. Normally, players make the manager; in this case the manager made the players. You know people always ask me about that time in 1969 when Gil walked all the way out to left field to take me out of the game. They wonder if I hold that against Gil. Well, at the time I was upset by it, sure. I was down a couple of days. But when I started to think about it I realized that there was a message there, not only for me, but for the whole team. Gil wanted 100 percent effort out of you all the time. If you couldn't or wouldn't give it, he didn't want you in the game. Hell, I was leading the league in hitting at the time. He did it with a definite purpose, and it worked, because right after that we went on a rampage.

You know, as you get older and look back, you realize a lot of things you didn't understand as a young player. There were times when I really didn't understand why Gil did the things he did. But now I look back and I realize what Gil was trying to teach us, not only as ballplayers, but as people. I think everybody who played for Gil will carry the lessons he taught them through their lives. If he had lived, he probably would have been the greatest manager who ever lived.

AL WEIS

Infielder, Played Under Hodges
1968–1971, New York Mets

Gil Hodges was sometimes a tough man to play for. In my career I played for three good managers: Al Lopez and Eddie Stanky with the White Sox, and Gil with the Mets, and I learned a lot from all three of them. But the difference in my case was that Gil gave me confidence in myself. He let me hit in certain situations during the course of the '69 season and World Series where, before that, I probably would have been taken out for a pinch hitter. I think that was one of the big things he did for his players; he built up their confidence.

He was just an outstanding man. I remember Gil and I always had this thing going when they played the National Anthem. He was an old Marine and I was in the Navy. So during the anthem both of us would stand at absolute attention. Neither one of us would start moving until the thing was completely over. Whenever I was out on the field I'd look over into the dugout, and there he was standing at attention. I think this tells you a lot about the man, too. Because Gil Hodges was a very patriotic and dedicated person.

DON CARDWELL

Pitcher, Played Under Hodges
1968–1970, New York Mets

I always had great respect for Gil even when I was playing against him, and then later when I played for him. He was head and shoulders above any other manager I ever played for. He was always looking ahead two or three innings; he knew what was coming up. I never played for another manager who was so into the game, who thought that far ahead.

He was a father figure to all those younger guys on the club. It was different for me because I was the old man on the pitching staff. I think Gil looked to me to assume a leadership role with the younger pitchers. We never really talked about it, but I think Gil wanted me in that role, so I tried to stay close to these guys.

Gil had a unique way of communicating. If somebody had screwed up the night before, Gil would get around to talking to that person the next day; but he usually did it on the field. He wouldn't say anything in the clubhouse in front of anybody to embarrass the player. Gil would just kind of work his way around to that player and have a little conference with him on the field. That was Gil's way. He was just a great man.

ART SHAMSKY

Outfielder, Played Under Hodges
1968–1971, New York Mets

Gil Hodges was a very quiet manager, much in the mold of Walter Alston. Very quiet, but a very, very strong man both emotionally and physically. He had a way of saying things to you by not saying anything to you, if you know what I mean. He wouldn't embarrass a player or yell at him in front of anybody else. I only saw him get really mad a couple of times in the four years I played for him.

He was the strong, silent type and everybody who played for him, I think, respected him. Maybe some of us didn't agree with him, but we always respected him. In my case I wish I had played more. He platooned me and I felt I could have played every day, and I used to get upset because I wanted more playing time. But that didn't upset Gil; he respected it. He wanted all his players to have that kind of attitude, wanting to play as much as they could.

I didn't talk to Gil that much, so I wasn't as close to him as some of the other players; but I will say this, history will show that Gil Hodges was a great manager.

TOMMIE AGEE

Outfielder, Played Under Hodges
1968–1971, New York Mets

Gil Hodges was a great manager, especially for me. He stuck by me during the hard times. He brought me over from the American League where he had seen me at my best, and even though I had a bad season in 1968 he stayed with me. He felt if I played up to my potential I could help the team win a championship, which is exactly what happened.

I think I would have played in the big leagues longer if he hadn't died because of the kind of relationship we had. He had a big impact on my life and I miss him. But I know he's in Heaven.

ED CHARLES

Third Baseman, Played Under Hodges 1968–1969, New York Mets

I was one of the first players on the Mets in 1968 to publicly praise Gil Hodges for his managerial abilities, as well as for the type of man he was. I had seen him manage in the American League and I recognized right away that he was very skillful and had the potential to become one of the game's great managers. I think one of his greatest assets was his ability to motivate players. That's what managing is all about, and Gil was one of the all-time greats at getting the best out of his players. I think one of the greatest impressions he made on me was when he started the platoon system in New York in 1968. The local writers and news media started giving him hell because the team was still losing. There was also some grumbling from the players who didn't like the way Gil was using them. But Gil didn't waver. He stuck to his guns. That's saying a helluva lot about a manager, especially in New York. You know what the media pressure is like in New York. But it didn't affect him. He'd read what the writers had to say, then he'd crumple it up and throw it in the trash. That impressed me as far as leadership goes. He stuck to his plans; not the media's plans, not the players' plans, but his. And pretty soon we started winning.

Another thing that really impressed me about Gil was the way he immediately established who was the boss. He let his men know right away who was in charge. You did things his way or you didn't play. That's important, especially with a young team like the Mets were.

The one thing Gil would not tolerate was guys who didn't hustle or put out. See, Gil's policy was simple. If you were sick or injured and you couldn't play, he wouldn't put you in the game no matter what you said. If you had an injury and didn't tell him he would get mad about that. When you went out there you had to give 100 percent. He didn't want you to cheat yourself, the team or the fans.

A perfect example of this is the Cleon Jones incident in 1969. You remember, when Cleon didn't hustle after a ball in left; so Gil walked all the way out to left field and took him out of the game. It turns out Cleon's leg was hurting him and he shouldn't have been in there to begin with. But he told Gil he could play. But when Gil saw that he didn't hustle after the ball the way he should have, he went out there to left field to get him. It took a lot of guts for Gil to do that, but he was telling everybody something. If you wouldn't or couldn't give your best, then you were not going to play. A lot of managers, when their star player pulls something like that, would have turned the other way and backed off. Not Hodges. And at that time Jones was hitting around .350 and leading the league. But that didn't matter to Gil. He was giving the team a message.

I remember another time when Jim McAndrew was pitching. A ball was hit toward first and McAndrew didn't get off the mound to cover the bag. This was in the first inning, but it didn't matter. Gil walked to the mound, stuck out his hand for the ball, and sent McAndrews to the showers. After that you can bet that every time a ball was hit to the right side our pitchers got over to that first base bag in a hurry.

You see, by doing these things he was telling the guys something. When you hit that field your mind's going to be on the game, you're going to be alert, and you're going to give 100 percent. Now, if you get everybody on the team thinking like this, you're going to develop a winning attitude, and that's what Hodges did with the Mets.

Gil Hodges was a fair man. Everybody on the club was equal from the first guy to the 25th guy. No exceptions. But he handled each player differently depending on his personality. He was a master at it. He could read people and he knew what made them tick. The players had total confidence in him. They knew what he did was going to be right. That's saying a helluva lot, when you can get 25 players to have total confidence in a manager. Let's face it, you're dealing with men who have reached the major league level, so they know a little something about the game. So if you have a manager who wavers or is indecisive they're going to sense that right away, and they're not going to respond. But Gil had that great combination of being decisive and knowing exactly what he was doing. The players responded to that. Maybe there was some grumbling when Gil initiated his platoon system, but he stuck to his guns and we started winning. Shortly after that all the moaning and bitching ceased. Suddenly everybody realized that we had a shot at going all the way, and from that point on all that mattered was winning.

There was only one time when I got angry at Gil. One day he pinch-hit for me in a crucial situation and I got peeved. I always felt I was at my best with the game on the line. So when I came back to the dugout I slammed my bat into the rack and stalked off into the clubhouse. Gil was sitting right there. All the guys looked over because it was very seldom that they'd see me get peeved like that. When I cooled down I realized it was a very bad thing for me to do, especially around the younger players. I showed Gil up and I shouldn't have. He expected me to set an example and I had let him down. I felt real bad about that.

The next day I came to the ball park and I walked over to all the younger players and I said, "You saw what I did yesterday when I was pinch-hit for? That was a bush thing for me to do. It was horseshit. I apologize to you guys because it was the wrong thing to do." Then I walked into Gil's office. He looked at me and said, "Ed, I knew you were coming. I know what kind of man you are." He didn't have to say another word and neither did I. We communicated without talking. We just smiled at each other.

I was a veteran when I played for Gil, but he taught me a lot. The lessons he taught his players went beyond the baseball field. He taught them lessons in life. How to conduct yourself as a gentleman, as a big leaguer. How to be a better person. There were just so many things Gil taught all of us.

His death was a terrible and tragic thing. It was a great, great loss. We lost in Gil Hodges one of the greatest human beings the game has ever known. Even now I think about him all the time. He had such an effect on all of us that I'm sure we'll all carry with us the lessons he taught us for the rest of our lives. I think if any of the men who played for Gil had the chance to say something to him, they'd say thank-you. Thank-you for the great memories. Thank-you for the World Championship you led us to. Thank-you for the lessons you taught us. Thank-you for everything, Gil, thank-you. . . .

"If you had a son, it would be a great thing to have him grow up to be just like Gil Hodges."

—Pee Wee Reese

"He was the quiet man, a great silent strength. I always felt Gilly was someone could turn to and rely on."

—Clem Labin

"I heard DiMaggio booed at Yankee Stadium. I heard Musial booed in St. Louis. never heard Gil booed anywhere. That speaks volumes for the kind of man he was.

—Carl Erskin

I think Gil Hodges presents everything that America has tried to teach young men about growing up and reaching manhood."

—Frank Howard

"With Gil, you knew that the family came first and he communicated that to his players."

—Bud Harrelson

"I'm grateful to have had the privilege of knowing him, and that he was part of my life."

—Don Drysdale

"Gil Hodges is a Hall of Famer; he deserves it, and it's a shame his family and friends have had to wait so long."

—Duke Snider

"Gil taught us all lessons we will carry with us the rest of our lives."
—Jerry Koosman

"You will never know how big a role Gil played in the lives of his players. They loved him and appreciate what he did for them as players and as men."

—Rube Walker

PART SIX

Back Home in Petersburg

SIX

He never forgot where he came from

I flew into the Louisville Airport on the Friday of Kentucky Derby weekend. It's the most important weekend of the year in that town. The city is consumed by it. As passengers arrive in the terminal, they are greeted by elegant young women dressed in silk hoopskirts handing out chocolate bon-bons, flavored, or course, with genuine Kentucky bourbon. As you pass the baggage claim area a country string band plays blue grass music. It was a wonderfully festive atmosphere, and the Derby was the talk of the town. But I wasn't in Louisville to attend "the run for the roses" at Churchill Downs. I was there only to rent a car to drive out of Kentucky into Indiana to visit Petersburg, the hometown of Gil Hodges.

To get to Petersburg from Louisville you drive about 100 miles west on Interstate 64 through the heart of southern Indiana. It is beautiful country, rolling green hills dotted with farmhouses and silos. One sees immense fields of crops and livestock grazing on the hills adjacent to the highway. As on any other interstate, the bucolic scene is marred by fast-food joints, gas stations, service areas and motels. But on certain portions of this highway, with country music playing on the car radio, you can almost believe you have been transported back in time to a simpler, more peaceful America.

About 20 miles from the Illinois border, you leave Interstate 64 and head north on Indiana Route 57, which leads to
Petersburg. Just a few miles off the interstate it is a different
world. Farms line the sides of the road and you can gaze
upon fields of brightly colored wildflowers. Here you don't
see the trappings of a commercialized America. But here and
there the landscape is scarred by coal mines, huge, open pits
with tractors of all shapes and sizes ripping the fossilized fuel
from the earth. This has been coal country as far back as
anybody can remember. Mining is different now. These days
they mine the coal from topside. They dig down from the
surface and strip it from the hillsides. The pay is better than
it was; there are unions to protect the workers; conditions
are much safer and there are benefits and insurance. What's
more, once the coal is taken, the coal companies are required
by law to reclaim the land, to fill in the pits and plant trees
and grass.

When Gil Hodges' father, Charlie, worked the mines in the
1930s, 40s and early 50s, conditions weren't so good. Back
then they traveled down into the earth. Charlie Hodges
worked the deep mines around Elberfeld, Indiana. There
were no unions then, no benefits or insurance; it was just
back-breaking, dangerous, killing work. And if a man was
hurt or could no longer work the mines, his family might just
starve. A life in the mines helped to kill Charlie Hodges at 54
years of age. But there wasn't much else for a man to do to
feed his family. Then, as now, most men in this part of the
country made their living in the mines or on a farm.

Traveling 25 miles north on route 57 delivers you right on
to Main Street In Petersburg. As you enter the town you are
greeted by a sign that says, "Welcome to Petersburg, Home
Town of Gil Hodges." The town's appearance hasn't
changed all that much since Gil grew up here. If the modern
cars were replaced by period vehicles, it would look like the
Twenties all over again. The Citizens Bank is a modern
building, and there are, of course, traffic and street lights,
and on the edge of town are mini-marts, gas stations and two

supermarkets. But downtown—the three blocks or so of Main Street—remains for the most part as it's always been. Lining both sides of the street are stores and businesses housed in brick buildings erected in the late 1800s.

Times are tough in Petersburg. It's never been easy. To make a living off the land or in the mines one must be tough, determined, resilient, words that describe Petersburg as well. Sometimes even these qualities aren't enough. In the past few years shopping malls have sprung up within driving distance of Petersburg, and a number of stores and businesses on Main Street, unable to compete, have closed down. There are thriving farms around Petersburg, but there are also those having a tough go of it, as are farmers throughout the Midwest. And if you're not born to a farm, land is expensive these days. There're always the coal mines, and the power plant that employs about 350 people, but it takes more than these to sustain a town of almost 3000 people; and young people leave for the cities to find work. What's happening now in Petersburg is happening in small towns all across America. A way of life is, sadly, vanishing.

*   *   *

THE PETERSBURG CITY HALL IS IN AN OLD BANK building on Main Street. Downstairs, below police headquarters, is where all the business of the town is conducted. I walked in and was greeted by Mayor Jack Kinman, with whom I had previously spoken on the phone. In the large back room of City Hall the mayor has gathered a group of men who knew Gil Hodges, who grew up with him. Four of these men, plus the mayor, were on the seven-man committee that had worked to name a northern Pike County bridge "The Gil Hodges Memorial Bridge." The other two members of that committee, Father Larry Vieck and Roddy Boger, have since passed away.

Eddie Hawkins is in his sixties and was a good friend and classmate of Hodges. The mayor himself graduated Petersburg High a year behind Gil. Bill Thomas, also in his sixties, is a retired businessman; for years he ran the dry cleaning shop in town. Bob Harris is the town funeral director. His family has owned the funeral home in Petersburg for over a century. A few years younger than the other men, he knew Hodges in later years when Gil would return home to visit his mother. Bob King is the town barber, has been since 1950. He was a close friend of the Hodges family. Also present is young Randy Harris, the newscaster at the local FM radio station and a passionate baseball fan.

In Petersburg Gil Hodges is known to everybody as "Bud." From the time he was a small child his mother and father called him "Buddy," and the name stuck. When the townspeople talk of Bud, it is with deep pride and warmth. They feel fortunate and proud to call him their own. "Sometimes the people over in Princeton claim that Princeton is really Bud's hometown because he was born there," says Mayor Kinman. "But Bud grew up right here in Petersburg."

"That's right," adds Bill Thomas. "They moved here from Princeton when Bob and Bud were no more than seven or eight."

I felt comfortable and completely at ease in the back room of the Petersburg City Hall. Being Brooklyn born and raised, my background could not have been more different from that of the men I sat with. But Gil Hodges was a bond between us. Talking and reminiscing about Gil made the conversation flow easily.

"You know, we used to have these excursions to Sportsman's Park in St. Louis to watch Gil play back in the Fifties," recalls Mayor Kinman. "The Petersburg Jay Cees sponsored it. It was my partner, Wendal Kinman, said. 'Why don't we buy a watch or something for Bud and present it to him at the ball park in St. Louis?' Well, we all thought that was a good idea. So that's what we did that first year. We got 50 tickets at first, but those went like nothing. Then we started ordering them in increments of 50 and the next thing you know, 458 people ended up going. The next year we had

passenger service on the B & O Railroad out of Washington,
Indiana, which is just a little north of here, and this time
about 1000 people made the trip. The third year we got 1300
to go. So in those three years 2,758 people made the trip to
see Bud play in St. Louis. Just about everybody in town was a
Dodger fan. About 99 percent of us, anyway. Sure, there
were some dyed-in-the-wool Cardinal fans, but this city
would have rooted for any team Bud played for; wouldn't
have mattered if it was Podunk."

"Would you say Gil had a real big effect on this town?" I
ask.

"Bud had just a tremendous effect on Petersburg," says
Bob Harris. "You really can't say exactly what it was. We
were just so proud of him and he generated so much
respect."

"I would say Bud had a big influence on us," replies the
mayor. "I remember during the off-season one year, Gil
came home to Petersburg for a visit. That year we had a real
good football team and we had won every game except for
the last, which we had to play against a tough team from
Mount Vernon. So we decided that at half time of that game
we were going to present Bud with a new shotgun and a set
of luggage. Well, half time came and we made the presenta-
tion. Then we went out and won that game 40-0. Now if you
think Bud's being here at the game had nothing to do with
that, you have another thing coming."

"Everybody in town always followed Gil," adds Bill
Thomas. "There was this fella named Vic Colvin had a dry-
cleaning store here in town. Every night he'd figure out
Bud's batting average and post it in the window of his shop
the next day. People used to stop by just to see how Bud was
doing. I'll tell you, Bud could do no wrong in this town. But
you know, when Bud came home, there wasn't a big fanfare
or nothing. He'd come back to see his mom, and then maybe
you'd see him on the street. Bud wasn't real outgoing. He
was always real quiet and reserved. His older brother Bob
was the outgoing one."

"You got that right," laughs Eddie Hawkins. "The difference between the two Hodges boys was night and day. Bob was just always running off at the mouth, and Bud was real quiet and reserved, just like his mom."

"That's right," says Bob King. "Bud's mom, Irene, was real quiet like Bud. She was the stabilizing influence in that family and Bud took after her. Now Bob, he took after his father, Charlie. Whenever Charlie Hodges was downtown you always knew he was there. He was just a-talking and a-talking all the time. Everybody liked him here in town. Ol' Charlie would be going in and out of stores talking about Bud and the Dodgers, just going a mile a minute."

"You remember when the Giants came back from all those games behind the Dodgers in 1951 to win the pennant? When Thomson hit that homer?" asks Mayor Kinman. "Well, I saw Charlie Hodges that day and he says to me, 'Yep, Branca threw that urineball and Thomson hit it.' I said 'Urineball, Charlie? What do you mean by that?' Charlie smiles and says, 'You know, Branca threw that urineball and Thomson smacked the piss out of it.' "

"Charlie Hodges worked them deep mines down by Elberfeld," recalls Ed Hawkins. "Conditions wasn't too good in them mines back then. Jeez, I can hear Charlie coughing yet. Just a-coughing and a-gagging all the time. You could hear him coming a mile away. He had real bad emphysema from working in those mines, and he was a chain smoker, too. He'd just light one cigarette after another. I used to say to him, 'Charlie, them cigarettes are going to kill you.' He'd say, 'I know, Eddie, I know, but you know how much I love my cigarettes.' Charlie worked hard in the mines, and it seemed there was always something wrong with him, broken bones and other injuries. But I'll tell you something, he always found time to play ball with his boys. He was always pitching to them."

"If you would have seen the two Hodges boys when they were growing up, you may have thought Bob was going to be the one who was going to make it," says Bill Thomas.

"Bob was just so enthusiastic about playing ball, and he looked like a big leaguer when he played. He had that form, you know? Bud was just as good, but he was so quiet you didn't notice him like you did Bob. But both of them were real good athletes."

"I remember a track meet we had one time," says Ed Hawkins. "Bud was a shot-putter and I ran the 440 relay. Anyway, on this particular day we were one man short on the relay team, so the coach says to Bud, 'Bud, you're going to run the 440 today.' Bud says, 'I can't do that. I never run a 440 in my life.' Coach says, 'Well, you're sure going to run one today.' Well, Bud ran it and I think we won, but Bud was sure winded after that race!

"Then there was one time when Bud broke the school shot-put record by over two feet," Hawkins continues. "I don't remember exactly how far he threw it, but it was past the old record by a good two feet. Anyway, the principal of the school takes the shot and brings it to the grocery store there by the high school to weigh it. Turns out the shot was light by an ounce or two, so the principal wouldn't count the record. Now, that wasn't fair at all. That shot should have been weighed on at least three scales and then you take the average of the three. But Ol' Bud, he was never able to throw it that far again."

"Yeah, but he always had a real strong arm," says Bill Thomas. "One year, right after the war, we had a pickup baseball team down here and Bud played a few games for us. He had just gotten out of the service. One day I was playing center field and Bud was playing third base. Round about the third inning our pitcher's arm gets sore; only thing is, we don't have another pitcher. So Bud says, 'I never pitched before, but I can throw pretty hard.' So Bud starts pitching. Catching that day was this small fella named Kenny Willis. Just a little guy; couldn't have weighed more than 135 pounds soaking wet. You have to understand that Bud had two pitches, fast and faster, and he just reared back and fired. The ball sounded like a rifle going off when it hit

Kenny's mitt. Well, we went ahead and won the game, and after it was over Kenny took off the catcher's glove and his left hand was about twice the size of his right. It was just all puffed up.''

"Hey Eddie," Bob Harris says to Ed Hawkins. "You know of any other classmates of yours who might know some stories about Bud?''

Ed thinks for a moment. "Hell, they're all dead or dying. They're ain't many of us left."

"How are things in Petersburg now?" I ask. "You know, the economy?''

"Terrible," answers Bob Harris.

"Just awful," says Bill Thomas.

"Well, it's not all that bad," says Mayor Kinman, ever the optimistic politician. "I think we have a lot of potential here. We're poor, but we have a lot of good people in Petersburg, and I think we can make it better. We have the power plant here that supplies Indianapolis with 80 percent of its power, and employs 350 people. We have another power plant that employs 50. We have to attract more industry to this area, and I think we have an untapped resource in the tourism area. Right now it's mostly farms and the mines, just like it's always been. But I think if the people work together we can do something about it. You know, back when each town had its own high school it was easier to get people together, because the high-school sports team kind of brought the whole town together. But, you know, Petersburg High has been torn down and now we have a central school for Pike County. It's a good school, and it makes sense economically, but it hurt us as far as getting the people of the town together. That's why I came out of retirement to become mayor. Some days I think I can do something, and other days, well, I don't know, it's tough."

"Economically we're not in that great a shape," says Randy Harris. He has sat through the whole conversation just listening to the stories about Gil. "I guess it's probably not that much different around here than when Gil Hodges was growing up.''

The men in the room nod in agreement.

"Hey, Mr. Mayor," says Ed Hawkins, adopting an official tone. "Can we do something about those signs that say this is Gil Hodges' hometown? They're pretty wore out, and them being green and white makes them pretty hard to read. Do you have a choice of the colors?"

"No, I don't," answers the mayor. "But since we don't have any money in the budget for new signs, maybe we can pass the hat around and repaint them."

"We have to do something about those colors," says Ed Hawkins. "Maybe we should paint them black and gold so you can see them better."

"Black and gold!" exclaims Bill Thomas. "Ed, what's the matter with you? Those are Purdue colors! Good God!"

"That's right," says Ed. "Strike that last remark. I don't know what got into me. Maybe we can paint them Indiana University colors, red and white."

Petersburg is Indiana University territory.

*   *   *

PETERSBURG, INDIANA, IS A TOWN WITH A LONG AND fascinating history. Pike County, where it lies, was the state's first official county, and Petersburg, the county seat, was established in 1820. Abraham Lincoln passed through these parts during his travels as a young man, and three houses in the town were used as "safe houses" for runaway slaves traveling north on the underground railroad.

Many of the buildings on Main Street, and a number of homes in town, were built in the mid-to-late 1800s; and many of the town's residents have heritages dating back to the pioneers who settled this area over 170 years ago. The people of Petersburg have a quiet respect for their history, but are not awed by it. Their history is a part of their makeup, a part of their everyday lives. Above all, they are practical, hardworking, honest people.

They have faced some tough times, and are facing them now; but they've always survived, even prospered at times.

They are not so very different from their ancestors who settled this valley. They are proud of what they have. Petersburg has two beautiful parks, and a movement is afoot to build a nine-hole golf course. This would bring people into town and certainly help the economy. But it takes a lot of money to build a golf course, and the town fathers are trying to figure out a way to raise the capital. There is town sentiment for putting commemorative plaques on the houses that were part of the underground railroad, but the money to do it just isn't in the town budget. There are more pressing problems to deal with.

The Petersburg area has a rich Indian heritage. Bordered on the north by the east fork of the White River, tribes of the Algonquian group lived here for centuries. These tribes were farmers and hunters, pushed west into southern Indiana by the stronger Iroquois. Because most of Pike County is still rural, the area is teeming with Indian artifacts.

In the basement of his home in Petersburg, Eddie Hawkins has the most extensive collection of Indian artifacts I have ever seen. "I've been collecting this stuff for over 60 years," he says. "It was my grandfather who got me started." The walls of his basement are lined with thousands of arrowheads; there are pottery pieces, weapons, necklaces, cooking utensils, tools and pipes. Some of his things date back to 400 B.C. "You don't even have to dig for this stuff," Ed tells me. "If you go along the banks of the river after a rain, or if you go through a farmer's field after he's just plowed, you'll find this stuff everywhere. Now I hear tell of some people digging up the Indian burial grounds. I don't think that's right. They're desecrating the Indians' sacred ground. That's like someone coming along digging up the graves of my ancestors. It's just not right."

Also in Ed's basement are miscellaneous pieces of memorabilia that have nothing to do with Indians. On the floor along one wall are numerous bricks from every building that has been torn down in Petersburg. On each brick is the date of the building's construction and demolition. On one wall hangs the rifle Ed's maternal grandfather used during the Civil War. One shelf contains a collection of campaign buttons from both local and national elections dating back to the Twenties. But the centerpiece of Ed's collection is a portrait of Gil Hodges. "A friend of mine gave me that," he says. "He was dying of cancer and he wanted me to have it. One day, sick and all, he got out of bed and came over here to give it to me. A couple of days later he died.

"This house we're standing in was built by my wife's father with his own two hands," Ed continues. "He worked in the mines for years, and every night he'd bring home a load of rock from the mines, and he used those rocks to build this house. Every night, after a day in the mines, he'd come and work on the house. Took him a lotta years, but he finished it. When I was a kid they hung a picture of this house on the bulletin board in my school and told how it was built. I thought it was just great. Little did I know that someday I would own and live in that house.

"When my wife was growing up here the Hodgeses lived just around the corner. My wife's father built a ping-pong table here in the basement, and a few nights a week a lot of the neighborhood kids would come down here to play, including the Hodges boys. Sometimes when I'm down here, I say to myself, 'Bud Hodges played ping-pong right here in my basement.' "

Eddie Hawkins stands proudly among a collection of Indian artifacts and other memorabilia. He is just as proud of the fact that Gil Hodges once played table tennis in his basement.

*　*　*

SETTLERS ORIGINALLY CAME TO PETERSBURG BEcause of fertile soil in the surrounding hills and the availability of water from the White River. It was a good land and a man could make himself a home if he was willing to work hard. Then coal was discovered in the earth and a whole new wave of people came to Petersburg to work the mines. Charlie Hodges came from the Princeton mines to work those in Petersburg in the early Thirties. With him he brought his wife, Irene, his two young sons, Bob, eight, and Bud, seven, and his three-year-old daughter Marjorie.

No one in Petersburg is quite sure where Charlie Hodges came from originally, nor do they know the ethnic origin of the Hodges name. "Charlie just showed up in Petersburg one day to work the mines," recalls Ed Hawkins. "His wife, Irene, was German; her name was Horstmeyer."

"Nobody knew where Dad originally came from," says Marjorie Hodges Maysent, Gil's younger sister. "His parents died when Dad was really young and he never talked about them. I knew that Mother's father was German and her mother was Irish, but none of us knew anything about Dad's people."

For most of their lives in Petersburg the Hodges family lived in two rented houses on Cherry Street. At first they lived in a small house with a tin roof, and later, when Charlie was doing a little better, they moved right next door to a bigger home. It wasn't until Bob and Bud graduated high school that Charlie was able to afford a home of his own, a big white house on East Main Street. It was the house Gil returned home to, the house his mother Irene lived in until the day she died. "I used to mow Mrs. Hodges' lawn for about five or six years." says 19-year-old Petersburg native Mike Hadley. "She was just a great lady. I really liked her. She was like a second grandmother to me. After I'd finish mowing the lawn she always had something for me to eat. She was such a nice lady; I was really upset when she died two years ago."

"Did she ever talk much about Gil?" I ask him.

"No, she was a pretty quiet lady, and I think talking about him probably upset her. But I remember one day I was sitting at her table eating and she said to me, 'Here Mike, I thought you might like to have this.' It was a baseball card of Gil.

Well, I can tell you that I have that card in a safe box at the bank.''

Just about everybody you speak to in Petersburg has a Gil Hodges story. On the first night I was there, Mayor Kinman, Randy Harris and I had dinner at Elmer's Restaurant on the outskirts of town. It was there I met Mrs. Chris Hadlock. "I remember when Gil came back for his grandmother's funeral," she reflects, sitting at our table. "She was in her nineties when she died. You know, in this little town, when someone dies, you bake a cake or something and bring it over to the family. So I made a cake to bring to the Hodgeses. I went over there and I brought my little girl with me. She has a crippled leg and was wearing a leg brace at the time. When we got there I introduced her to Gil. I said, 'This is Gil Hodges, Mrs. Hodges' son, the one we always watch play ball on television.' Well, my little girl looks up at him and says, 'So what?' Gil smiled and said, "I can see I've made a really big impression on her.' Well, do you know before we left that day she was sitting in his lap, and wanting him to go to school with her the next day so they could play. Gil said to her, 'I'd love to go to school with you, but I have to get back to play ball.'

"He was just a wonderful person, more like his mom than his dad. Now Charlie Hodges, he was just something else. One time I saw Charlie talking to somebody about Gil and the Dodgers, and he was describing a play Gil made, and he's waving his hands all over the place. Now Gil had given Charlie the new watch he was wearing that day, and as he's describing the play, his arms waving and all, that watch comes flying off his wrist and sails clear across the room. That's Charlie for you. I'll never forget that.''

A short time later a woman named Adra Green comes over to our table. She had heard us talking about Gil Hodges. "I remember when Gil came back here to go to college in Oakland City." she says. "He had just gotten married and he brought his wife down here with him. I was living in an apartment with a few other girls, and every morning we used to watch Gil as he walked to class. He was one of the most handsome fellows you'd ever want to see and us girls used to ogle him 'cause he was so good looking. His wife was real pretty, but we didn't see her too much. She didn't come out very often. We always used to wonder how she was taking it; you know, a big-city girl like that from Brooklyn coming to live in a small town in Indiana. I'm sure it was totally different from anything she was used to."

* * *

THE NEXT MORNING MAYOR KINMAN, BILL THOMAS, Ed Hawkins, Bob Harris and I met again at City Hall. The mayor thought it would be "a good base of operations." We are joined by Dave Johnson, the sports editor of the *Evansville Courier* and a big Gil Hodges fan, and by "Ol' Doc" Weathers. William "Doc" Weathers, now in his eighties, is somewhat of a legend himself in Petersburg. He was for many years principal of the high school, and he coached Bob and Bud Hodges when they were in junior high. "In junior high Bob and Bud were just little guys," recalls Doc. "Bud really didn't grow that much until he was in high school. Both boys were fine athletes, though. One time we went down to Princeton for a track meet and I told the Princeton coach, 'You see those two Hodges boys? They were born here in Princeton, but we have them now up in Petersburg and you're going to hear about those two.' They were small fellas then, but once you got them on the field they were both very competitive. I knew that Bud was going to be a great athlete, but back then I never thought that he'd become as great as he did."

"He should be in the Hall of Fame, that's how great he was," Dave Johnson adds. "You know, every year for a long time I'd write my why-Gil-Hodges-should-be-in-the-Hall-of-Fame column. I even sent some of those columns to members of the Veterans Committee at the Hall of Fame, but I don't know if that does any good.''

Johnson collects Gil Hodges memorabilia. He has brought with him a loose-leaf book full of 8 x 10 glossy photos of Gil taken throughout his career. There must be several hundred of them. As a young sportswriter Johnson had the opportunity to meet and talk with Gil on a number of occasions. Among his prize possessions are photos of him and Gil together. "It really broke me up when Gil died," he says sadly. "I admired the man so much."

"It was Father Vieck and Bob Harris went up to the funeral in Brooklyn when Bud died," says Bill Thomas.

"I wish you could have met Father Vieck; he was a great guy," the mayor says, and the other men in the room nod their heads in agreement. "He was a big Gil Hodges fan," the mayor continues. "Always kept in contact with Bud. Fact is, it was Father Vieck who was the chairman of the bridge committee. He was really the moving force behind getting the bridge named in Gil's honor. Father Vieck did a lot for this town. He really knew how to bring people together. Maybe now we're not as together as we should be, but it would have been different had Father Vieck lived. I wish you could have met him."

"Father Vieck and I went up to Gil's funeral, and neither of us had ever seen anything like it," says Bob Harris. "When we got to the airport we got a cab, and the cab driver says to us, 'Are you two going to the funeral?' Now how many cabs go to Brooklyn from LaGuardia Airport? But this driver could tell just by looking at us that we were in New York for the funeral. When we got to the church the line of people outside must've been at least three blocks long. And it wasn't single file; it was four or five people across. There were just thousands of people. That's how we found the church; we just followed the line. Inside the church, on the left side, were all the dignitaries from the ball clubs, at least two people from every team in both leagues. Plus there was a

multitude of baseball greats there, too, players like Joe Di-
Maggio and such. On the right side was the family, and also
there were all the little kids from the Gil Hodges Little
League, all these small fellas dressed in their baseball uniforms. It was something to see.''

"That was Easter Sunday when Bud died, if I remember,''
says Ed Hawkins. "A friend of mine calls me up and says he
just heard on the radio that Bud Hodges died of a heart attack
in Florida. Well, it really shook me up. It really did. Just took
it right out of me. Even when I get to thinking about it today
I still can't hardly believe it. He was just too young to die.
But he was the type that just never blowed up. Never let
anything out. Always kept it bottled up inside. I'm like that
myself and it's no good for you. I've had four heart attacks
and a stroke. I feel lucky just being able to sit here and talk to
you today. Bud, he was the same way, only he wasn't as
lucky as I been.''

"Maybe it would have been better if Bud was more like his
brother Bob; you know, more outgoing and such,'' says Bill
Thomas. "I remember, though, that Bob and Bud used to get
into it once and a while. They'd go at each other. One time
we were playing a pickup game over at Higgins' field. Jim
Higgins owned this field and we used to play there all the
time. Well, one day Bob and Bud got into it over something,
I forget exactly what. Anyway, Jim Higgins had boxing
gloves, so he comes out and says, "We'll just put the boxing
gloves on you two boys and settle this thing.'' So we put up a
ring for them, and they put on the gloves and went at it.
They just whacked it out.''

"Who won?'' I ask.

"Oh, Bud usually won. He was the stronger of the two.''

"I remember playing up there at Higgins','' says Wayne
Malotte, who has joined us at City Hall. A few years younger
than the Hodges boys, Malotte recalls that as a kid he looked
up to them as the star athletes of the town. "We used to use
cow pies for bases out there,'' he says. "Sometimes you'd go
running into a base and it'd be a little soft if the pie hadn't set

long enough. There was this one time a bunch of us smaller guys was playing up there and Bud Hodges came on over to the field. He says, 'Hey, all you little guys, come over here. I want you guys to throw the ball to me as hard as you can, and I'll catch it with my bare hands.' Well, all us kids just reared back and fired the ball as hard as we could and he caught every one of our throws with those big hands of his. He made it look so easy.''

"Bud was always like that," adds Bill Thomas. "He made everything he did look easy."

Later that morning Mayor Kinman, Bill Thomas and I took a ride around town. First we visited the three houses Gil had lived in while growing up in Petersburg, and then we rode out to the Gil Hodges Memorial Bridge. We parked the car on the opposite side of the road and crossed Route 57 to where the stone monument to Gil stands.

"Who thought of the wording on the monument?" I ask the mayor.

"Well, we all had some input," he says, "but it was really Father Vieck who came up with most of it. He really loved Gil. . . . You should have been here the day the bridge was dedicated," he continues with great pride in his voice. "There were about 2000 people here." Mayor Kinman points out a grass-covered area no larger than half an acre. "Everybody was just packed in. Governor Whitcomb flew down from Indianapolis by helicopter to be here. Gil, Jr. was down from Brooklyn, and of course Gil's mom was here and so was his brother Bob. Carl Erskine came down from Anderson, Indiana. It was sure something."

We stood for a moment looking at the monument.

"I wish we could have done more for Bud while he was alive," says the mayor. "We were all just so proud of him."

*　*　*

THE BARBER SHOP IN ANY SMALL TOWN IN AMERICA is a gathering place. Bob King's shop in Petersburg is no different. When I walked in my eyes were immediately drawn to the two barber chairs. They are a circular, deco design, fully upholstered and trimmed in bright silver metal with ashtrays in each arm. "I guess I got these chairs around 1950," says King. "They were top of the line back then. Don't think they make them like this anymore."

I'm sure he's right, and I'm thinking that some yuppie in New York would probably pay two grand each for these chairs to put in his rec room. In Petersburg, Bob King uses them to cut hair. "I gave Bud a haircut many times in these chairs," he says proudly.

The door to the shop opens and Mayor Kinman and Bill Thomas walk in. "I wonder where Eddie's at?" asks Bill. "He was supposed to meet us here. We drove around but we couldn't find him."

"I hope everything's okay," says the mayor. "Ed said something this morning about his wife not feeling too well. I hope she's okay."

"Hey Bill, you remember a pitcher from around here by the name of Don Liddle?" Bob asks. "I think he played for the Cardinals."

"Sure, he was a little left-hander with a good curve."

"Yep, that's him. Well, one summer when Bud was playing in an industrial league he had a game against Mount Carmel and this Liddle was pitching for them. I went with Bud across the river for the game, and the first two times up Bud struck out. Liddle had that good curve and Bud always had his problems with a good curveball. Third time up, though, Liddle got behind and had to bring one over. Well, Bud hit the damn thing so far, he just knocked the hell out of it. Of course, he always had good power."

"Yeah," says Bill Thomas, "Bud had the power but his brother Bob always had the form. You know, he looked real good out there. He had a perfect batting stance and he looked great when he was pitching. And at first base, being a lefty, he had all the moves down. He was always so enthusiastic, just talking it up all the time."

"Bob used to come in here all the time," recalls Bob King. "When he was working for that sporting goods store over in Evansville he used to supply the Petersburg little league with all their equipment. After the games he'd come in here, put all the bats and stuff in the back room, and just start talking. He never sat down. I can still see him pacing back and forth here, just a-talking and talking."

"Did everyone think that Bob might be the one to make it as a big leaguer?" I ask.

"Well, he was good, but Bud had the size," says Bob King. "Size is important and Bud was about six-one and weighed 170, 180. Bob was only five-ten and much lighter. But hell, I don't think anyone in this town ever dreamed of a career like the one Bud ended up having. It was just beyond your imagination. Nobody had any money back in those days, but you really didn't notice because everybody else was in the same boat. Only way I ever got a bicycle is because my sister bought me one. The Hodges boys, they only had one bike between them. It was pretty banged up and they just rode the shit out of that thing."

"I don't think Bud himself ever thought, when he was growing up, that he'd be a big leaguer," reflects Bill Thomas. "Like Bob said, it was just something that was beyond your imagination. Now, when you look back at it, you can see that Bud was always just a little better than the rest of us at everything."

"Sure was," Bob King says. "He always beat us at everything. He would study things. You might be playing ping-pong or pool and Bud would watch you and figure out your weaknesses, and then he'd know how to beat you. He was real quiet and shy and all, but he was always real competitive."

"I'd have to say, though, that Bud always enjoyed coming back home," Mayor Kinman says.

"I think so," agrees Bill Thomas. "Back right after he had his first heart attack he came home to rest up a little bit. I used to see him real early in the mornings taking a walk through town, just kind of strolling down Main Street."

"He used to do that even when he was playing for the Dodgers," remembers Bob King. "He could really relax when he came home. We all knew he was great and we admired him and all, but because we grew up with him, to us he was always the same Bud we had known all our lives. I can still see him walking down the street. He'd get up about six o'clock and walk through town, and then down to the field where we played Legion ball when we were kids. He'd walk around the infield, walk around the outfield, stand by the plate. He was probably thinking back to the days when we all played there, and how far he'd come since then."

The door to the barber shop opens and Eddie Hawkins and his wife come in.

"This here is my wife, Roma. She was one of Bud's girl friends."

"Oh, go on Ed," she says. "I was just a good friend. I wasn't his girl friend, although I wish I could have been. Bud was so handsome, but he was so shy. He used to walk through study hall in school and the girls would just wilt because he was so good looking."

"What is it you used to call him?" Ed asks his wife.

"Well, I remember we used to call him "Moon" because he had that big face, and we used to call him "Moose," too. I think another name we had for him was the "Cisco Kid," but I don't rightly know where we got that one, probably from the movie serial or maybe the radio program."

"The girls always liked Bud," says Bob King. "But back then Bud loved playing ball more than anything. I remember one time we had an American Legion game, but Bud couldn't play because he had a job delivering groceries and he had to work that day. He wanted to play so damn bad, but he would never miss work. Well, that day he went like mad delivering them groceries all over town just so he could get to the field. I'll never forget it. Bud shows up at the game still wearing his white apron from the grocery store and wanting to play."

"Charlie and Irene Hodges were really proud of both their boys," says Roma Hawkins.

"They sure were," says Bob King, smiling. "Of course they showed it in different ways. Charlie was always talking about his sons, especially when Bud was with the Dodgers. Irene was just as proud, but she didn't show it like Charlie did."

"The whole town was proud," says Mayor Kinman. "We all used to go to St. Louis as much as we could to watch Bud play."

"Charlie and Irene used to go over to St. Louis maybe two or three times a year," recalls Bob King. "Once and a while I'd go with them. Bud would meet us at the players' entrance with tickets for the game. Those were sure wonderful times."

*   *   *

LATER THAT SATURDAY AFTERNOON, AFTER BILL Thomas, Ed Hawkins and Mayor Kinman left, Bob King and I sat in his barber shop and talked about Gil.

"I remember something that happened to us just after the war," he says with a smile. "I guess it was in 1946 because Bud and I hadn't seen each other in three years with both of us being in the service. Well, on this particular Saturday night Bud had gotten Charlie's car and asked me if I wanted to take a ride over to Jasper. So we picked up this girl we both knew and we headed out. I think we maybe had a few beers in Jasper and after a while we decided to come home. Anyway, we're driving through this intersection in Jasper and this car comes out of nowhere and hits the right side of our car. None of us were hurt, and you could still drive it, but the car was smashed up pretty bad.

"So we all jump out of the car, and these young people from Jasper that hit us say we better call the police. Only thing is, they know all the policemen in town by their first names. I said to Bud, 'Hey Bud, I think we're in trouble because no matter who they call they're going to know him.' Bud says, 'Bob, I believe you're right.' So the police come, and sure enough we're the ones who get the ticket.

"When we got back to Petersburg, Bud went in to see his dad. He said, 'Dad, we had a wreck over in Jasper.' Now, Charlie Hodges could be a pretty explosive guy. But he didn't get mad or nothing. I think we was just so happy to have Bud back from the war nothing fazed him.

"Well, the girl we went to Jasper with, she worked over in Evansville, and she wanted to go back there Sunday night to be there for work Monday morning. So Bud borrows his dad's car again on Sunday, and the three of us head off to Evansville. We drop the girl off, and sure enough, as we're driving through an intersection there, this car comes out of the side street and hits the left side of the car. Now both sides of Charlie's car are smashed in. Boy, I felt so bad for Bud. This was the car Charlie used to go to work every day.

"Well, we got back to Petersburg about midnight, except Bud don't want to go home. He don't want to go home until his father gets up for work. Thing is, Charlie didn't get up until five in the morning and it was only twelve o'clock. So Bud and I spent the next five fours driving around town and talking. Finally, the light in the kitchen goes on and we go in. Irene is cooking Charlie's breakfast and getting his lunch ready, and Bud tells him what happened. I thought Charlie might explode this time, but he didn't. I felt so relieved for Bud because he was so worried. But Charlie was just so happy to have Bud home safe from the war that the car being wrecked on both sides just didn't matter."

The next morning, Sunday, Bob King and I had breakfast in a place called Jerry's in Oakland City, about 13 miles south of Petersburg. Oakland City, as a sign at the edge of town informs you, is the hometown of Hall of Famer Edd Roush.

"When Bud was home he used to eat breakfast at the place we're going to quite often," says Bob King as we drive south on Route 57. "This would be the way Bud would have come. I can recall that Bud took his wife Joan here to eat a few times. She didn't come to Petersburg more than a couple of times that I can remember. She may have been here more, but I only saw her a couple of times."

We pull into the parking lot of Jerry's. "This place wasn't called Jerry's when Bud came here," Bob King says. "I don't remember exactly what the name was, but Bud was here a lot."

Inside, after ordering breakfast, Bob talks about his friend. "Thing about Bud was, he was always so smooth no matter what he did. He had that style about him, even when he was a kid. There used to be this nightclub out there where the bridge is now. It didn't serve liquor or nothing, just soft drinks, but it had a jukebox and a ping-pong table and dancing. Sometimes a group of us would go down there to play ping-pong and dance. You should have seen Bud dance. He was just so graceful. It just came natural to him. Hell, everything Bud did seemed to come natural to him. I remember we used to go bird hunting together. I grew up on a farm in the country so I went hunting quite a bit, and I thought I was a pretty good shot. Bud, he grew up in town, so he didn't go hunting all that much. But when we went out there, he was one of the best shots you ever saw. So smooth and steady. I thought I was good, but I was nowhere near as good as Bud. That was the thing with him. He was always a step ahead of the rest of us."

* * *

THAT SUNDAY AFTERNOON I DROVE TO THE HOME of Bob Harris. He lives in a big, beautiful house on a hill, one of the nicest homes in Petersburg. After a while Mayor Kinman arrived, anxious to see the video tape Bob Harris was going to show me. The tape contained a transfer of a black and white film that someone had taken in downtown Petersburg during the early summer of 1940.

Watching this film was to look back in time; to get a glimpse of a different America. On this particular Saturday in 1940, Main Street is crowded with people. Cars, parked head-in, line both sides of the street. Coal miners, in town for the day, are evident everywhere. Farmers and their families are dressed up for their big day in town. Business is booming in all the stores and shops.

We watch the flickering images of a vanished America. Bob Harris and Mayor Kinman recognize people and buildings that have vanished from the scene. There is an underlying sadness in their voices as they reminisce about times gone by, about the last period of innocence before the Second World War. Many of the young men we see in the film were called to arms only a year after this film was shot. These young men saw the horror and bloodshed of war, and some of them never returned home. They died thousands of miles away from the rolling green hills and deep mines of Petersburg, their names now carved in stone on a town monument that also features the names of those who died in the Civil War and the First World War.

"You know what really strikes me about that film," says Mrs. Harris after it's over. "The people look happy. You can tell just by looking at their faces that they're happy."

Bud Hodges was one of the lucky ones who returned home to Petersburg after the war. But the life he had known before the war was gone forever, and soon thereafter he would leave Petersburg. He never talked about his war experiences, not even to his closest friends in his hometown. "I remember just one time when Gil mentioned something to somebody," says Bob Harris. "I think he was referring to Iwo Jima, and he said, 'All you did was duck your head and pray.' "

On the table in the Harris living room are two boxes filled with Gil Hodges memorabilia. Two scrap books contain clippings from throughout Gil's baseball career. In one of these are letters Gil wrote home to Father Vieck. I read them. Often Gil asked the priest to say a prayer for his mother, Irene. In others, Gil says that he'd sure like to get away from New York and do some hunting down around home.

Bob's son-in-law hands me a stack of documents from Hodges' baseball career. I look through them. I see Gil's official release from the Los Angeles Dodgers in 1961, enabling him to sign with the expansion New York Mets. I look over Gil's contract with the 1962 Mets. It calls for a salary of $39,500. A letter from Dodger vice-president Buzzy Bavasi makes it clear that Gil is having some difficulty dealing with Mets general manager George Weiss over his salary for 1962. Buzzy will do what he can to help, but says, "I guess some organizations aren't as generous as the Dodgers." Then I see Gil's official notification of release as manager of the Washington Senators so he can sign to manage the Mets in 1968. I read Gil's three-year managerial contract with the Mets. It's much shorter than his player's contract, but he made substantially more money—$50,000 per year—to manage the Mets than to play for them. A few moments later Mrs. Harris walks into the living room holding a frame. It contains one of the most remarkable pieces of baseball memorabilia I have ever seen. It is a newspaper photo of the original members of the Baseball Hall of Fame who were living at the time of their induction in 1939—Babe Ruth, Honus Wagner, Walter Johnson, Eddie Collins, Connie Mack, Cy Young, Napoleon Lajoie, Tris Speaker, Grover Cleveland Alexander, George Sisler and Rogers Hornsby—and it is autographed by each of them. The only living inductee missing from this legendary photo is Ty Cobb. He was late getting to Cooperstown that day.

"I imagine that's worth something," Bob Harris says to me.

"It's worth thousands," I say. "I can't tell you exactly how much, but I wouldn't be surprised if it was the only one of its kind in existence."

Whenever the subject of the Hall of Fame comes up in Petersburg, the same question is always asked. How come Gil Hodges hasn't been inducted?

"Gil Hodges belongs in the Hall of Fame," says Bob Harris. "How can he not be in? When he retired he had more homers than any other right-handed hitter in National League history. He made the All-Star team eight times. He was a big reason why the Dodgers won six pennants in the

14 years he played with them. He hit more than 20 homers 11 times, had seven seasons of more than 100 RBIs; he hit 14 grand slams, and hit four homers in a game, which only eight other guys have done in all of baseball history. Plus when you take into account what he did as a manager and the kind of man he was, I just can't understand it."

I have no answers for Bob Harris.

*   *   *

ON MONDAY MORNING, MY LAST DAY IN PETERSBURG, I went to the Dairy Queen for breakfast. Bill Thomas and Bob King came in only a few minutes after I arrived.

"So, have you enjoyed yourself here in Petersburg?" Bill asks.

"I sure have. I've had a great time." And I did. I admire and respect these people. They are sincere, generous people, and one feels in them a sense of strength and purpose. They are facing some tough times these days. They've faced them before. One feels they'll survive.

It is easy to understand, after spending time in Petersburg, Indiana, why Gil Hodges became the man he did; why he held the values and beliefs he did.

"You know, I think Bud had a good life," says Bob King. "He died young and that's sad. He had so much to give. He was such a good person. But no matter how famous Bud got, I think in his own mind he always thought of himself as just Bud Hodges from Petersburg, Indiana. He never forgot where he came from."

Later that morning I dropped by City Hall to say good-bye to Mayor Kinman. As I got in my car to leave town, I decided to take one last ride out to the Gil Hodges Memorial Bridge. I parked the car and walked over to the stone monument. I stood there and once again read of Gil's many accomplishments. When the monument was erected in 1972, the bridge committee decided to leave a blank space toward the bottom of the stone on which the words from Gil's Hall of Fame plaque would be carved.

Eighteen years have passed and the space at the bottom of the stone remains blank.

Petersburg, Indiana, as it appeared in May of 1990, a month before a tornado destroyed much of the town.

The sign as you enter Petersburg says it all.

Petersburg High, Class of 1941. Gil Hodges is in the top row, fourth from the left.

The Petersburg track team of 1941. Gil is in the middle row, fourth from the right.

he St. Joseph's College
rsity basketball team in
942. Gil is number 29 on
e far right in the bottom
w.

il as a varsity football
layer at St. Joseph's in
942.

The Hodges home on East Main Street in Petersburg, Indiana.

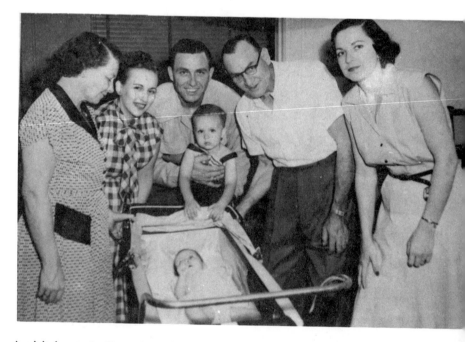

A visit home to Petersburg in the Fifties. *Left to right;* Gil's mother Irene, wife Joan, Gil (holding Gil, Jr.) father Charlie, sister Marjorie and Gil's daughter Irene in the carriage.

e Gil Hodges Memorial Bridge, spanning the East Fork of the White River in
rthern Pike County, Indiana.

e sign on the Petersburg side of the Gil Hodges Bridge.

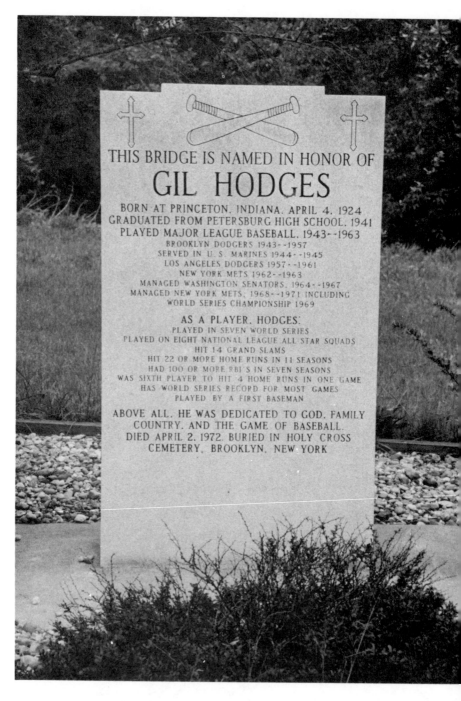

THIS BRIDGE IS NAMED IN HONOR OF

GIL HODGES

BORN AT PRINCETON, INDIANA, APRIL 4, 1924
GRADUATED FROM PETERSBURG HIGH SCHOOL, 1941
PLAYED MAJOR LEAGUE BASEBALL, 1943--1963
BROOKLYN DODGERS 1943--1957
SERVED IN U.S. MARINES 1944--1945
LOS ANGELES DODGERS 1957--1961
NEW YORK METS 1962--1963
MANAGED WASHINGTON SENATORS, 1964--1967
MANAGED NEW YORK METS, 1968--1971 INCLUDING
WORLD SERIES CHAMPIONSHIP 1969

AS A PLAYER, HODGES:
PLAYED IN SEVEN WORLD SERIES
PLAYED ON EIGHT NATIONAL LEAGUE ALL-STAR SQUADS
HIT 14 GRAND SLAMS
HIT 22 OR MORE HOME RUNS IN 11 SEASONS
HAD 100 OR MORE RBI'S IN SEVEN SEASONS
WAS SIXTH PLAYER TO HIT 4 HOME RUNS IN ONE GAME
HAS WORLD SERIES RECORD FOR MOST GAMES
PLAYED BY A FIRST BASEMAN

ABOVE ALL, HE WAS DEDICATED TO GOD, FAMILY
COUNTRY, AND THE GAME OF BASEBALL,
DIED APRIL 2, 1972, BURIED IN HOLY CROSS
CEMETERY, BROOKLYN, NEW YORK

The stone monument that stands in a field next to the Gil Hodges Bridge. The emp
space at the bottom was reserved for the words on Gil's Hall of Fame plaque, s
blank eighteen years after his death.

APPENDICES

GIL HODGES' PLAYING RECORD

BORN: Apr. 4, 1924, Princeton, Ind. HT: 6-2; WT: 200;

RESIDENCE: Brooklyn, N.Y. Former first baseman.

YEAR CLUB	G	AB	R	H	2B	3B	HR	RBI	AVG
1943-Brooklyn	1	2	0	0	0	0	0	0	.000
1944-45				(In Military Service)					
1946-Newport News	129	406	65	113	27	7	8	64	.278
1947-Brooklyn	28	77	9	12	3	1	1	7	.156
1948-Brooklyn	134	481	48	120	18	5	11	70	.249
1949-Brooklyn	156	596	94	170	23	4	23	115	.285
1950-Brooklyn	153	561	98	159	26	2	32	113	.283
1951-Brooklyn	158	582	118	156	25	3	40	103	.268
1952-Brooklyn	153	508	87	129	27	1	32	102	.254
1953-Brooklyn	141	520	101	157	22	7	31	122	.302
1954-Brooklyn	154	579	106	176	23	5	42	130	.304
1955-Brooklyn	150	546	75	158	24	5	27	102	.289
1956-Brooklyn	153	550	86	146	29	4	32	87	.265
1957-Brooklyn	150	579	94	173	28	7	27	98	.299
1958-Los Angeles (NL)...	141	475	68	123	15	1	22	64	.259
1959-Los Angeles (NL)...	124	413	57	114	19	2	25	80	.276
1960-Los Angeles (NL)...	101	197	22	39	8	1	8	30	.198
1961-Los Angeles (NL)...	109	215	25	52	4	0	8	31	.242
1962-Mets	54	127	15	32	1	0	9	17	.252
1963-Mets	11	22	2	5	0	0	0	3	.227
Major League Totals.....	2071	7030	1105	1921	295	48	370	1274	.273

WORLD SERIES RECORD

YEAR CLUB	G	AB	R	H	2B	3B	HR	RBI	AVG
1947-Brooklyn	1	1	0	0	0	0	0	0	.000
1949-Brooklyn	5	17	2	4	0	0	1	4	.235
1952-Brooklyn	7	21	1	0	0	0	0	1	.000
1953-Brooklyn	6	22	3	8	0	0	1	1	.364
1955-Brooklyn	7	24	2	7	0	0	1	5	.292
1956-Brooklyn	7	23	5	7	2	0	1	8	.304
1959-Los Angeles	6	23	2	9	0	1	1	2	.391
World Series Totals......	39	131	15	35	2	1	5	21	.267

ALL-STAR GAME RECORD

YEAR LEAGUE	AB	R	H	2B	3B	HR	RBI	AVG
1949-National	3	1	1	0	0	0	0	.333
1950-National-a								
1951-National	5	2	2	0	0	1	2	.400
1952-National-a								
1953-National	1	0	0	0	0	0	0	.000
1954-National	1	0	0	0	0	0	0	.000
1955-National	1	0	1	0	0	0	0	1.000
1957-National	1	0	0	0	0	0	0	.000
All-Star Game Totals	12	3	4	0	0	1	2	.333

a-Selected; did not play

GIL HODGES' MANAGERIAL RECORD

Gil Hodges
HODGES, GILBERT RAYMOND
B. Apr. 4, 1924, Princeton, Ind.
D. Apr. 2, 1972, West Palm Beach, Fla.

		G	W	L	PCT		
1963 WAS A		122	42	80	.344	10	10
1964		162	62	100	.383	9	
1965		162	70	92	.432	8	
1966		159	71	88	.447	8	
1967		161	76	85	.472	6	
1968 NY	N	163	73	89	.451	9	
1969		162	100	62	.617	1	
1970		162	83	79	.512	3	
1971		162	83	79	.512	3	
9 yrs.		1415	660	754	.467		

Your full home address. *1421. E. Main. St. Petersburg, Indiana* Phone No. *174-J*

BASEBALL RECORD

Club		Year	Position	Batting Average	If Pitcher Won-Lost
1st Professional	*Brooklyn*	2 mos. *1943*	*C. 4. 3B*	*.000*	....
2nd Professional	....	....	....	....	....
3rd year, etc.	....	....	....	....	....
....	....	....	....	....	....
....	....	....	....	....	....
....	....	....	....	....	....
....	....	....	....	....	....
....	....	....	....	....	....
....	....	....	....	....	....

Draft Status. *Discharged* .... Date. *February. 27. 1946*

     The undersigned grants to the National League of Professional Baseball Clubs, the right to consent to the use of his photograph and above information for publicity purposes as may in its judgment seem desirable, with stipulation that s may in no instance be used as an endorsement of any product, nor carry any advertising matter.

(signed) *Gilbert Ray Hodges*

NOTE: If the answers to any of these questions require more space than is provide please use another sheet of paper. Publicity is important to any player, to his club and to the National League. Detailed replies to questions concerning early phase of your career will be helpful in assisting baseball writers who are interested in your story.

                        Arthur E. Patterson

AFTER HIS DISCHARGE FROM THE ARMY, GIL SIGNED A RELEASE — REQUIRED OF ALL PLAYERS — SO HIS PICTURE COULD BE USED FOR PUBLICITY.

NOTICE TO PLAYER OF RELEASE OR TRANSFER
NATIONAL LEAGUE

October 10 , 19 61

Mr. GILBERT R. HODGES

You are hereby notified as follows:

~~That your contract has been unconditionally released~~
That your contract has been assigned to the Metropolitan Baseball
Club of National League.

(a) *Without right of recall.*

(b) ~~With right of recall.~~

(Cross out parts not applicable. In case of optional agreement, specify all conditions affecting player.)

LOS ANGELES DODGERS, Inc.,

Corporate Name of Club.

Vice President.

Copy must be delivered to player; also forwarded to President of League of which Club is a member, and to the Commissioner.

GIL'S OFFICIAL NOTICE OF THE TRANSFER OF HIS CONTRACT FROM THE
LOS ANGELES DODGERS TO THE EXPANSION NEW YORK METS.

LOS ANGELES DODGERS, INC.
EXECUTIVE OFFICES, LOBBY FLOOR, HOTEL STATLER
930 WILSHIRE BOULEVARD
LOS ANGELES 17, CALIFORNIA
MADISON 3-1261

January 11, 1962

Mr. Gilbert R. Hodges
3472 Bedford Avenue
Brooklyn, New York

Dear Gil:

I talked to George Weiss today and I guess other clubs are
not as generous as the Dodgers. Gil, you sat here in my
office last year and you said to me "if you are traded to
one of the new clubs and should be cut, would the cut be
based on the $44,000. or the figure in my contract" and I
told you on the higher figure.

It seems to me this is a matter for you and I to discuss -
your actual contract negotiations have nothing to do with
this. You get as much as you can - but keep in mind had
you stayed with the Dodgers, I am sure you felt you could
not be paid the same as you had been getting.

I have no intention of getting into your salary problems
with the "Mets" but I do want you to know whatever you and
I agreed upon, still stands. We may have to go a few rounds
but everything will come out alright.

Regards.

Very truly yours,

E. J. Bavasi

EJB:ew

IT IS OBVIOUS IN THIS LETTER FROM BUZZIE BAVASI THAT GIL WAS HAVING SOME PROBLEMS
IN HIS CONTRACT NEGOTIATIONS WITH GEORGE WEISS AND THE METS. THE DODGERS HAD
RELEASED HIM A FEW MONTHS BEFORE TO PLAY FOR THE ORIGINAL METS IN 1962.

NEW YORK NATIONAL LEAGUE BASEBALL CLUB
OPERATED BY
METROPOLITAN BASEBALL CLUB INC.

POLO GROUNDS
ESS OFFICE: AU. 6-8400
TICKET OFFICE
AU 6-1010

EXECUTIVE OFFICES
680 FIFTH AVENUE
NEW YORK 19, N. Y.
LT 1-2300

February 12, 1962

Mr. Gilbert Ray Hodges
3472 Bedford Avenue
Brooklyn, New York

Dear Gil:

    Attached please find copy of your 1962 contract with

the New York Mets.

    Best of luck this coming season.

                              Sincerely,

                              John J. Murphy
                              Administrative Assistant

JJM:t
Enc.

___

JOHNNY MURPHY'S COVER LETTER THAT ARRIVED WITH GIL'S 1962 CONTRACT.

"MEET THE METS"

UNIFORM PLAYER'S CONTRACT

National League of Professional Baseball Clubs

Parties Between METROPOLITAN BASEBALL CLUB, INC.

herein called the Club, and GILBERT RAY HODGES

of BROOKLYN, NEW YORK , herein called the Player.

Recital The Club is a member of the National League of Professional Baseball Clubs, a voluntary ass of ten member clubs which has subscribed to the Major League Rules with the American League of sional Baseball Clubs and its constituent clubs and to the Professional Baseball Rules with that Lea the National Association of Baseball Leagues. The purpose of those rules is to insure the public wh and high-class professional baseball by defining the relations between Club and Player, between cl club, between league and league, and by vesting in a designated Commissioner broad powers of cont discipline, and of decision in case of disputes.

Agreement In consideration of the facts above recited and of the promises of each to the other, the partie as follows:

Employment 1. The Club hereby employs the Player to render, and the Player agrees to render, skilled servic

baseball player during the year .... 196.....
including the Club's training season, the Club's exhibition games, the Club's playing season, and the Series (or any other official series in which the Club may participate and in any receipts of which the may be entitled to share).

Payment 2. For performance of the Player's services and promises hereunder the Club will pay the Pla sum of $39,500 (Thirty Nine Thousand Five Hundred) per wording on page 3

In semi-monthly installments after the commencement of the playing season covered by this c unless the Player is "abroad" with the Club for the purpose of playing games, in which event the amou due shall be paid on the first week-day after the return "home" of the Club, the terms "home" and " meaning respectively at and away from the city in which the Club has its baseball field.

If a monthly rate of payment is stipulated above, it shall begin with the commencement of the playing season (or such subsequent date as the Player's services may commence) and end with the ter of the Club's scheduled playing season, and shall be payable in semi-monthly installments as above p

If the player is in the service of the Club for part of the playing season only, he shall receive s portion of the sum above mentioned, as the number of days of his actual employment in the Club' season bears to the number of days in said season.

Notwithstanding the rate of payment stipulated above, the minimum rate of payment to the Pl each day of service on a Major League Club shall be at the rate of $6,000 per year; except that such r rate of payment shall be at the rate of $7,000 per year retroactive to the beginning of the season if the is on a Major League Club's roster on June 15 and shall be at the rate of $7,000 per year if the physically joins a Major League Club between June 15 and August 31. If a player physically joins League Club on or after September 1, the minimum rate of payment shall be at the rate of $6,000 for each day of service with such Major League Club.

Loyalty 3. (a) The Player agrees to perform his services hereunder diligently and faithfully, to keep hi first class physical condition and to obey the Club's training rules, and pledges himself to the America and to the Club to conform to high standards of personal conduct, fair play and good sportsmanship.

Baseball Promotion (b) In addition to his services in connection with the actual playing of baseball, the Player a cooperate with the Club and participate in any and all promotional activities of the Club and its which, in the opinion of the Club, will promote the welfare of the Club or professional baseball, observe and comply with all requirements of the Club respecting conduct and service of its teams players, at all times whether on or off the field.

Pictures and Public Appearances (c) The Player agrees that his picture may be taken for still photographs, motion pictures or t at such times as the Club may designate and agrees that all rights in such pictures shall belong to and may be used by the Club for publicity purposes in any manner it desires. The Player further ag during the playing season he will not make public appearances, participate in radio or television prog permit his picture to be taken or write or sponsor newspaper or magazine articles or sponsor co products without the written consent of the Club, which shall not be withheld except in the reasonab ests of the Club or professional baseball.

Player Representations 4. (a) The Player represents and agrees that he has exceptional and unique skill and ability as a player; that his services to be rendered hereunder are of a special, unusual and extraordinary characte gives them peculiar value which cannot be reasonably or adequately compensated for in damages at that the Player's breach of this contract will cause the Club great and irreparable injury and damag

Ability Player agrees that, in addition to other remedies, the Club shall be entitled to injunctive and other relief to prevent a breach of this contract by the Player, including, among others, the right to en Player from playing baseball for any other person or organization during the term of this contract.

Condition (b) The Player represents that he has no physical or mental defects, known to him, which would or impair performance of his services.

Interest in Club (c) The Player represents that he does not, directly or indirectly, own stock or have any interest in the ownership or earnings of any Major League club, except as hereinafter expressly s and covenants that he will not hereafter, while connected with any Major League club, acquire or l such stock or interest except in accordance with Major League Rule 20 (e).

Service 5. (a) The Player agrees that, while under contract, and prior to expiration of the Club's right this contract, he will not play baseball otherwise than for the Club, except that the Player may parti post-season games under the conditions prescribed in the Major League Rules. Major League Rule is set forth on page 4 hereof.

her
orts

(b) The Player and the Club recognize and agree that the Player's participation in other sports may impair or destroy his ability and skill as a baseball player. Accordingly the Player agrees that he will not engage in professional boxing or wrestling; and that, except with the written consent of the Club, he will not engage in any game or exhibition of football, basketball, hockey or other athletic sport.

6. (a) The Player agrees that this contract may be assigned by the Club (and reassigned by any assignee Club) to any other club in accordance with the Major League Rules and the Professional Baseball Rules.

(b) The amount stated in paragraph 2 hereof which is payable to the Player for the period stated in paragraph 1 hereof shall not be diminished by any such assignment, except for failure to report as provided in the next sub-paragraph (c).

(c) The Player shall report to the assignee Club promptly (as provided in the Regulations) upon receipt of written notice from the Club of the assignment of this contract. If the Player fails so to report, he shall not be entitled to any payment for the period from the date he receives written notice of assignment until he reports to the assignee Club.

(d) Upon and after such assignment, all rights and obligations of the assignor Club hereunder shall become the rights and obligations of the assignee Club; provided, however, that

(1) The assignee Club shall be liable to the Player for payments accruing only from the date of assignment and shall not be liable (but the assignor Club shall remain liable) for payments accrued prior to that date.

(2) If at any time the assignee is a Major League Club, it shall be liable to pay the Player at the full rate stipulated in paragraph 2 hereof for the remainder of the period stated in paragraph 1 hereof and all prior assignors and assignees shall be relieved of liability for any payment for such period.

(3) Unless the assignor and assignee clubs agree otherwise, if the assignee Club is a National Association Club, the assignee Club shall be liable only to pay the Player at the rate usually paid by said assignee Club to other players of similar skill and ability in its classification and the assignor Club shall be liable to pay the difference for the remainder of the period stated in paragraph 1 hereof between an amount computed at the rate stipulated in paragraph 2 hereof and the amount so payable by the assignee Club.

(e) If this contract is assigned by a Major League Club to another Major League Club during the playing season, the assignor Club shall pay the Player, for all moving and other expenses resulting from such assignment, the sum of $300 if the contract is assigned between Clubs in the same zone; the sum of $600 if the contract is assigned between a Club in the Eastern Zone and a Club in the Central Zone; the sum of $900 if the contract is assigned between a Club in the Central Zone and a Club in the Western Zone; and the sum of $1,200 if the contract is assigned between a Club in the Eastern Zone and a Club in the Western Zone. The Eastern Zone shall include the Philadelphia, New York and Pittsburgh clubs in the National League and the Baltimore, Boston, New York and Washington clubs in the American League; the Central Zone shall include the Chicago, Cincinnati, Milwaukee, St. Louis and Houston clubs in the National League and the Chicago, Cleveland, Detroit, Kansas City and Minnesota Twins clubs in the American League; the Western Zone shall include the Los Angeles and San Francisco clubs in the National League and the Los Angeles club in the American League.

If this contract is assigned by a Major League Club to a National Association Club during the playing season, the assignor Club shall pay the Player his reasonable and actual moving expenses resulting from such assignment and shall reimburse the Player for up to one month's rental payments for living quarters in the city of the assignor Club for which he is legally obligated after the date of such assignment and for which he is not otherwise reimbursed.

(f) All references in other paragraphs of this contract to "the Club" shall be deemed to mean and include any assignee of this contract.

7. (a) The Player may terminate this contract, upon written notice to the Club, if the Club shall default in the payments to the Player provided for in paragraph 2 hereof or shall fail to perform any other obligation agreed to be performed by the Club hereunder and if the Club shall fail to remedy such default within ten (10) days after the receipt by the Club of written notice of such default. The Player may also terminate this contract as provided in sub-paragraph (f)(4) of this paragraph 7.

(b) The Club may terminate this contract upon written notice to the Player (but only after requesting and obtaining waivers of this contract from all other Major League Clubs) if the Player shall at any time:

(1) fail, refuse or neglect to conform his personal conduct to the standards of good citizenship and good sportmanship or to keep himself in first class physical condition or to obey the Club's training rules; or

(2) fail, in the opinion of the Club's management, to exhibit sufficient skill or competitive ability to qualify or continue as a member of the Club's team; or

(3) fail, refuse or neglect to render his services hereunder or in any other manner materially breach this contract.

(c) If this contract is terminated by the Club by reason of the Player's failure to render his services hereunder due to disability resulting directly from injury sustained in the course and within the scope of his employment hereunder and written notice of such injury is given by the Player as provided in the Regulations on page 4 hereof, the Player shall be entitled to receive his full salary for the season in which the injury was sustained, less all workmen's compensation payments paid or payable by reason of said injury.

(d) If this contract is terminated by the Club during the training season, payment by the Club of the Player's board, lodging and expense allowance during the training season to the date of termination and of the reasonable traveling expenses of the Player to his home city and the expert training and coaching provided by the Club to the Player during the training season shall be full payment to the Player.

(e) If this contract is terminated by the Club during the playing season, then, except in the case provided for in sub-paragraph (c) of this paragraph 7, the Player shall be entitled to receive as full payment hereunder such portion of the amount stipulated in paragraph 2 hereof as the number of days of his actual employment in the Club's playing season bears to the total number of days in said season, provided, however, that if this contract is terminated under sub-paragraph (b) (2) of this paragraph 7 for failure to exhibit sufficient skill or competitive ability, the Player shall be entitled to an additional amount equal to thirty (30) days payment at the rate stipulated in paragraph 2 hereof and the reasonable traveling expenses of the Player to his home.

(f) If the Club proposes to terminate this contract in accordance with sub-paragraph (b) of this paragraph 7, the procedure shall be as follows:

(1) The Club shall request waivers from all other Major League clubs. Such waiver request must state that it is for the purpose of terminating this contract and it may not be withdrawn.

(2) Upon receipt of the waiver request, any other Major League club may claim assignment contract at a waiver price of $1.00, the priority of claims to be determined in accordance with the League Rules.

(3) If this contract is so claimed, the Club shall, promptly and before any assignment, not Player that it had requested waivers for the purpose of terminating this contract and that the c had been claimed.

(4) Within 5 days after receipt of notice of such claim, the Player shall be entitled, by notice to the Club, to terminate this contract on the date of his notice of termination. If the fails so to notify the Club, this contract shall be assigned to the claiming club.

(5) If the contract is not claimed, the Club shall promptly deliver written notice of terminat the Player at the expiration of the waiver period.

(g) Upon any termination of this contract by the Player, all obligations of both parties hereunde cease on the date of termination, except the obligation of the Club to pay the Player's compensa said date.

Regulations
8. The Player accepts as part of this contract the Regulations printed on the fourth page hereof.

Rules
9. (a) The Club and the Player agree to accept, abide by and comply with all provisions of the League Rules and the Professional Baseball Rules which concern player conduct and player-club relatio and with all decisions of the Commissioner and the President of the Club's League, pursuant thereto.

Disputes
(b) In case of dispute between the Player and the Club, the same shall be referred to the Commi as an arbitrator, and his decision shall be accepted by all parties as final; and the Club and the Player that any such dispute, or any claim or complaint by either party against the other, shall be presented Commissioner within one year from the date it arose.

Publication
(c) The Club, the League President and the Commissioner, or any of them, may make public the fi decision and record of any inquiry, investigation or hearing held or conducted, including in such rec evidence or information, given, received or obtained in connection therewith.

Renewal
10. (a) On or before January 15 (or if a Sunday, then the next preceding business day) of th next following the last playing season covered by this contract, the Club may tender to the Player a c for the term of that year by mailing the same to the Player at his address following his signature heret none be given, then at his last address of record with the Club. If prior to the March 1 next succeedin January 15, the Player and the Club have not agreed upon the terms of such contract, then on or bel days after said March 1, the Club shall have the right by written notice to the Player at said address to this contract for the period of one year on the same terms, except that the amount payable to the Playe be such as the Club shall fix in said notice; provided, however, that said amount, if fixed by a Major Club, shall be an amount payable at a rate not less than 75% of the rate stipulated for the precedin

(b) The Club's right to renew this contract, as provided in subparagraph (a) of this paragra and the promise of the Player not to play otherwise than with the Club have been taken into consid in determining the amount payable under paragraph 2 hereof.

11. This contract is subject to federal or state legislation, regulations, executive or other official or other governmental action, now or hereafter in effect respecting military, naval, air or other govern service, which may directly or indirectly affect the Player, Club or the League and subject also to th of the Commissioner to suspend the operation of this contract during any national emergency.

Commissioner
12. The term "Commissioner" wherever used in this contract shall be deemed to mean the Commi designated under the Major League Agreement, or in the case of a vacancy in the office of Commi the Executive Council or such other body or person or persons as shall be designated in the Major Agreement to exercise the powers and duties of the Commissioner during such vacancy.

Supplemental Agreements
The Club and the Player covenant that this contract fully sets forth all understandings and agre between them, and agree that no other understandings or agreements, whether heretofore or hereafter shall be valid, recognizable, or of any effect whatsoever, unless expressly set forth in a new or supple contract executed by the Player and the Club (acting by its president, or such other officer as sha been thereunto duly authorized by the president or Board of Directors, as evidenced by a certifica of record with the League President and Commissioner) and complying with the Major League Rul the Professional Baseball Rules.

Special Covenants

Player is to be paid a sum of $30,000. (Thirty Thousand Dollars), during the playing season of 1962. The additional $9,500. payable under this contract, will be paid during the baseball season of 1964.

Approval
This contract or any supplement hereto shall not be valid or effective unless and until approved League President.

Signed in duplicate this .... 30th .... day of .... January ...., A. D. 1

Gilbert Ray Hodges
(Player)

3472 Bedford Ave, Brooklyn N.Y.
(Home address of Player)

Metropolitan Baseball Club, Inc

By _George M. Weiss_
President   (Authorized Signa

Social Security No. ....

Approved .... FEB 2 1962 ....196.......,

Warren Giles

President, National League of Professional Baseball Clubs

REGULATIONS

1. The Club's playing season for each year covered by this contract and all renewals hereof shall be as fixed by the National League of Professional Baseball Clubs, or if this contract shall be assigned to a Club in another league, then by the league of which such assignee is a member.

2. The Player, when requested by the Club, must submit to a complete physical examination at the expense of the Club, and if necessary to treatment by a regular physician or dentist in good standing. Upon refusal of the Player to submit to a complete medical or dental examination the Club may consider such refusal a violation of this regulation and may take such action as it deems advisable under Regulation 5 of this contract. Disability directly resulting from injury sustained in the course and within the scope of his employment under this contract shall not impair the right of the Player to receive his full salary for the period of such disability or for the season in which the injury was sustained (whichever period is shorter), together with the reasonable medical and hospital expenses incurred by reason of the injury and during the term of this contract, less all workmen's compensation payments paid or payable by reason of said injury; but only upon the express prerequisite conditions that (a) written notice of such injury, including the time, place, cause and nature of the injury, is served upon and received by the Club within twenty days of the sustaining of said injury and (b) the Club shall have the right to designate the doctors and hospitals furnishing such medical and hospital services. Any other disability may be ground for suspending or terminating this contract at the discretion of the Club.

3. The Club will furnish the Player with two complete uniforms, exclusive of shoes, the Player making a deposit of $30 therefor, which deposit will be returned to him at the end of the season or upon the termination of this contract, upon the surrender of the uniforms by him to the Club.

4. The Club will pay all proper and necessary traveling expenses of the Player while "abroad," or traveling with the Club in other cities, including board, lodging, Pullman accommodations, if available, and during the training season, an allowance of $25 per week, payable in advance, to cover other training trip expenses. The Club will also pay the reasonable traveling expenses of the Player to his home at the end of the season.

5. For violation by the Player of any regulation or other provision of this contract, the Club may impose a reasonable fine and deduct the amount thereof from the Player's salary or may suspend the Player without salary for a period not exceeding thirty days, or both, at the discretion of the Club. Written notice of the fine or suspension or both and of the reasons therefor shall in every case be given to the Player.

6. In order to enable the Player to fit himself for his duties under this contract, the Club may require the Player to report for practice at such places as the Club may designate and to participate in such exhibition contests as may be arranged by the Club for a period beginning not earlier than February 15 in 1947 and not earlier than March 1 in 1948 and subsequent years without any other compensation than that herein elsewhere provided, the Club, however, to pay the necessary traveling expenses, including Pullman accommodations, if available, and meals en route, of the Player from his home city to the training place of the Club, whether he be ordered to go there direct or by way of the home city of the Club. In the event of the failure of the Player to report for practice or to participate in the exhibition games, as provided for, he shall be required to get in playing condition to the satisfaction of the Club's team manager, and at the Player's own expense, before his salary shall commence.

7. In case of assignment of this contract the Player shall report promptly to the assignee club within 72 hours from the date he receives written notice from the Club of such assignment, if the Player is then not more than 1600 miles by most direct available railroad route from the assignee Club, plus an additional 24 hours for each additional 800 miles.

Post-Season Exhibition Games. Major League Rule 18 (b) provides:

Exhibition Games. (b) No Player shall participate in any exhibition game played during the period between the close of the Major League championship season and the following training season; except that a Player, with the written consent of the Commissioner, may participate in exhibition games which are played within thirty days after the close of the Major League championship season and which are approved by the Commissioner. Player conduct, on and off the field, in connection with such post-season exhibition games shall be subject to the discipline of the Commissioner. The Commissioner shall not approve more than three Players of any one Club on the same team. No Player shall participate in any exhibition game with or against any team which, during the current season or within one year, has had any ineligible player or which is or has been during the current season or within one year, managed and controlled by an ineligible player or by any person who has listed an ineligible player under an assumed name or who otherwise has violated, or attempted to violate, any exhibition game contract; or with or against any team which, during said season or within one year, has played against teams containing such ineligible players, or so managed or controlled. Any player violating this rule shall be fined not less than fifty dollars ($50) nor more than five hundred dollars ($500), except that in no event shall such fine be less than the consideration received by such player for participating in such game.

DISTRICT OF COLUMBIA STADIUM
22nd and East Capitol Streets
WASHINGTON, D. C. 20003

October 17, 1967

TELEPHONES
EXECUTIVE OFFICE 546-2880
TICKET OFFICE   544-1900

*National Game from
the Nation's Capital*

Mr. Gilbert R. Hodges
3472 Bedford Avenue
Brooklyn, New York

Dear Gil:

Enclosed is your official notice of release by
The Senators, Inc. as of October 11, 1967.

With very best wishes for success in your new
position from the entire organization I am,

Sincerely,

George A. Selkirk
General Manager

GAS:hp
Encl: Official Notice No. A1994
cc: Charles M. Segar, Joseph E. Cronin (with enclosures)
CERTIFIED MAIL NO. 360697

LETTER FROM WASHINGTON GENERAL MANAGER GEORGE SELKIRK
NOTIFYING GIL OF HIS RELEASE FROM WASHINGTON SO HE COULD
SIGN TO MANAGE THE METS.

No. **A** 1994

NOTICE TO ~~PLAYER~~ OF RELEASE OR TRANSFER

MANAGER

AMERICAN LEAGUE

................October 11................, 19 67...

Γo Mr. **Gilbert Ray Hodges**

You are hereby notified as follows:

1. *That you are unconditionally released.*

~~That your contract has been assigned to the~~ XXXXXXXXXXXXXXXXXXXXXX
~~XXXXXXXXXXXXXXXXXXXXXX League.~~   (a) *Without right of recall.*

~~XXXXXXXXXXXXXXXXXXXX~~

Released outright and unconditionally.

(Cross out parts not applicable. In case of optional agreement, specify all conditions affecting player.)

THE SENATORS, INC.

Corporate Name of Club

General Manager   XXXXX

☞ Copy must be delivered to player; also forwarded to President of League of which Club is a member and to the Commissioner.

GIL'S OFFICIAL NOTICE OF RELEASE AS THE MANAGER OF THE SENATORS ON OCTOBER 11TH, 1967, THE SAME DAY HE SIGNED A THREE-YEAR CONTRACT TO MANAGE THE NEW YORK METS.

NEW YORK NATIONAL LEAGUE BASEBALL CLUB

SHEA STADIUM, FLUSHING, N.Y. 11368

November 6, 1967

OHN J. MURPHY
CE PRESIDENT

Mr. Gilbert Ray Hodges
3472 Bedford Avenue
Brooklyn, New York 11210

Dear Mr. Hodges:

Mr. Murphy is in St. Petersburg, Florida, and has
asked me to send your approved copy of 1968 contract
with the Mets (including 69 & 1970).

Best of luck for the '68 season, and if there is any
information you require, please do not hesitate to call
Mr. Murphy.

Sincerely,

Rose Trotta

Secretary to
John J. Murphy
Vice President

Encl.

LETTER SENT BY JOHNNY MURPHY'S OFFICE WITH GIL'S THREE-YEAR CONTRACT TO MANAGE
THE METS.

National League of Professional Baseball Clubs

UNIFORM MANAGER'S CONTRACT

Parties

The **METROPOLITAN BASEBALL CLUB.,INC.**

herein called the Club, and **GILBERT RAY HODGES**

of **BROOKLYN, NEW YORK** , herein called the Manager.

Recital

The Club is a member of the National League of Professional Baseball Clubs. As such, and jointly with the other members of the League, it is a party to agreements and rules with the American League of Professional Baseball Clubs and its constituent clubs, and with the National Association of Professional Baseball Leagues. The purpose of these agreements and rules is to insure to the public wholesome and high-class professional baseball by defining the relations between clubs and their employes, between club and club, between league and league, and by vesting in a designated League President and Commissioner broad powers of control and discipline, and of decision in case of disputes.

Agreement

In consideration of the facts above recited, the parties agree as follows:

Employment

1. The Club hereby employes the Manager to render skilled service as such in connection with all baseball activities of the Club during the year **68, 69, and 70** the Manager covenants that he will perform with diligence and fidelity the service stated and such duties as may be required of him by the Club.

Salary

2. For the service aforesaid the Club will pay the manager an aggregate salary of $ **50,000.**
Fifty Thousand Dollars **Per Season** as follows:

In semi-monthly installments after the commencement of the playing season covered by this contract, unless the Manager is "abroad" with the Club for the purpose of playing games, in which event the amount then due shall be paid on the first week-day after the return "home" of the Club, the terms *"home"* and *"abroad"* meaning, respectively, *at* and *away from* the city in which the Club has its baseball field. If the Manager is in the service of the Club for part of the playing season only, he shall receive such proportion of the salary above mentioned, as the number of days of his actual employment bears to the number of days in the Club's playing season.

Loyalty

3. (a) The Manager pledges himself to the American public to conform to high standards of personal conduct, of fair play and good sportsmanship.

(b) The Manager represents that he does not, directly or indirectly, own stock or have any financial interests in the ownership or earnings of any Major League club, except as hereinafter expressly set forth, and covenants that he will not hereafter, while connected with any Major League club, acquire or hold any such stock or interest except in acccordance with Major League Rule 20(e).

Service

4. The Manager shall not render baseball service during the period of this contract otherwise than for the Club.

Agreements and rules

5. (a) The National League Constitution and the Major League and Professional Baseball Agreements and Rules, and all amendments thereto hereinafter adopted, are hereby made a part of this contract, and the Club and Manager agree to accept, abide by and comply with the same and all decisions of the League President or Board of Directors and of the Commissioner, pursuant thereto.

Publication

(b) It is further expressly agreed that, in consideration of the rights and interest of the public, the Club, the League President, and/or the Commissioner may make public the record of any inquiry, investigation or hearing held or conducted, including in such record all evidence or information given, received or obtained in connection therewith, and including further the findings and decisions therein and the reasons therefor.

Special Covenants

6. This contract is subject to Federal or State legislation, regulations, executive or other official orders, or other governmental action, now or hereafter in effect, respecting Military, Naval, Air or other governmental service, which may, directly or indirectly, affect the Manager, the Club or the League; and subject also to all rules, regulations, decisions or other action by the Major Leagues, the Commissioner, the Major League or Professional Baseball Advisory Council, or the League President, including the right of the Commissioner to suspend the operation of this contract during any National emergency.

7. The Club and Manager covenant that this contract fully sets forth all understandings and agreements between them, and agree that no other understandings or agreements, whether heretofore or hereafter made, shall be valid, recognizable, or of any effect whatsoever, unless expressly set forth in a new or supplemental contract executed by the Manager and the Club (acting by its president, or such other officer as shall have been thereunto duly authorized by the president or Board of Directors, in writing filed of record with the League President and Commissioner — and that no other Club officer or employee shall have any authority to represent or act for the Club in that respect), and complying with all agreements and rules to which this contract is subject.

This contract shall not be valid or effective unless and until approved by the League President.

Signed in duplicate this _____11ᵗ_____ day of _____October_____, A. D. 19_67_

(SEAL)

Witness:

Metropolitan Baseball Club., Inc.
(Club)

By _____
(President)

Gilbert Ray Hodges
(Manager)

3472 Bedford Ave., Brooklyn, N.Y.
(Address of Manager)

The NATIONAL LEAGUE OF
PROFESSIONAL BASEBALL CLUBS
CAREW TOWER
CINCINNATI 2, OHIO

October 20, 1967

Dear Gil:

Welcome back "home" to the National League.
As I told you at Boston, we're all so glad to have a
gentleman of your stature and ability, and proud
you are to be one of our managers.

As you know, you are with a fine, progressive
organization where the Met fan interest is really a
baseball phenomenon.

Again, welcome - we're proud to have a real
National Leaguer managing a National League club.

Anything I or my staff can do to help at any
time please call on us.

Very sincerely yours,

Warren C. Giles
President

Mr. Gil Hodges
Manager, New York Mets
Shea Stadium
Flushing, N.Y. 11368

NEW YORK METS DAY-BY-DAY RECORD

1969 BASEBALL SEASON

Date	Vs.	W-L	Score	Winning Pitcher	Losing Pitcher	Team Record	Pos.	GB
4-8	Mtl	L	10-11	Shaw	Koonce	0-1	4(T)	1
4-9	Mtl	W	4-2	McGraw	Stoneman	1-1	3(T)	1
4-10	Mtl	W	9-5	Gentry	Jaster	2-1	3	2
4-11	StL	L	5-6	Carlton	Koosman	2-2	3	2
4-12	StL	L	0-1	GIUSTI	CARDWELL	2-3	3(T)	2
4-13	StL	L	1-3	GIBSON	Seaver	2-4	4(T)	3
4-14	At Pha	L	1-5	FRYMAN	McAndrew	2-5	5(T)	4
4-15	At Pha	W	6-3	Gentry	Wagner	3-5	4(T)	4
4-16	At Pit	L	3-11	MOOSE	Koosman	3-6	5	5
4-17	At Pit	L	0-4	Bunning	Cardwell	3-7	5	6
4-19	At StL	W	2-1	SEAVER	GIBSON	4-7	4(T)	6
4-20	At StL	W	11-3	Ryan	Briles	5-7	3(T)	5½
4-21	Pha	L	1-2(11)	Fryman	Taylor	5-8	3(T)	6
4-23	Pit	W	2-0	KOOSMAN	Bunning	6-8	3(T)	4½
4-25	Chi	L	1-3	JENKINS	Seaver	6-9	4	5
4-26	Chi	L	3-9	HANDS	Cardwell	6-10	5	6
4-27	Chi	L	6-8	Regan	Koonce	6-11	6	7
4-27	Chi	W	3-0	McGraw	NYE	7-11	4(T)	6
4-29	At Mtl	W	2-0	Ryan	Grant	8-11	3(T)	6½
4-30	At Mtl	W	2-1	SEAVER	WEGENER	9-11	3	5½
5-1	At Mtl	L	2-3	Face	CARDWELL	9-12	4	6
5-2	At Chi	L	4-6	Holtzman	Gentry	9-13	5	7
5-3	At Chi	L	2-3	Regan	Koonce	9-14	5	8
5-4	At Chi	W	3-2	SEAVER	Hands	10-14	4	7
5-4	At Chi	W	3-2	McGRAW	Selma	11-14	4	6
5-6	Cin	W	8-1	CARDWELL	Nolan	12-14	4	6
5-7	Cin	L	0-3	Merritt	Gentry	12-15	4	6
5-10	Hou	W	3-1	SEAVER	Lemaster	13-15	3	5
5-11	Hou	L	2-4	DIERKER	Cardwell	13-16	3	6
5-11	Hou	W	11-7	Koonce	D. Wilson	14-16	3	5½
5-13	Atl	L	3-4	R. Reed	Gentry	14-17	3	7
5-14	Atl	W	9-3	Seaver	P. Niekro	15-17	3	7
5-15	Atl	L	5-6	Jarvis	Cardwell	15-17	3	7½
5-16	At Cin	W	10-9	Koonce	Culver	16-18	3	7½
5-17	At Cin	W	11-3	GENTRY	Maloney	17-18	3	6½
5-21	At Atl	W	5-0	SEAVER	P. Niekro	18-18	3	5½
5-22	At Atl	L	3-15	Jarvis	McGraw	18-19	3	6½
5-23	At Hou	L	0-7	GRIFFIN	Gentry	18-20	4	7½
5-24	At Hou	L	1-5	DIERKER	Koosman	18-21	4	8½
5-25	At Hou	L	3-6	Lemaster	Seaver	18-22	4	9
5-27	SD	L	2-3	SANTORINI	McAndrew	18-23	4	9
5-28	SD	W	1-0(11)	McGraw	McCool	19-23	4	9
5-30	SF	W	4-3	Seaver	Linzy	20-23	4	9
5-31	SF	W	4-2	Gentry	Perry	21-23	3	9
6-1	SF	W	5-4	Taylor	Gibbon	22-23	3	9
6-2	LA	W	2-1	KOOSMAN	Osteen	23-23	3	8½
6-3	LA	W	5-2	Seaver	Foster	24-23	2	8½
6-4	LA	W	1-0(15)	Taylor	Mikkelsen	25-23	2	8½
6-6	At SD	W	5-3	Gentry	Ross	26-23	2	8½
6-7	At SD	W	4-1	KOOSMAN	Podres	27-23	2	8
6-8	At SD	W	3-2	Seaver	Santorini	28-23	2	7½
6-10	At SF	W	9-4	Cardwell	McCormick	29-23	2	7
6-11	At SF	L	2-7	PERRY	Gentry	29-24	2	7
6-13	At LA	L	0-1	FOSTER	Koosman	29-25	2	8½
6-14	At LA	W	3-1	Seaver	Sutton	30-25	2	8½
6-15	At LA	L	2-3	Drysdale	DiLauro	30-26	2	8½
6-17	At Pha	W	1-0	GENTRY	Champion	31-26	2	7
6-17	At Pha	L	3-7	G. JACKSON	Cardwell	31-27	2	7
6-18	At Pha	W	2-0	KOOSMAN	Wise	32-27	2	6
6-19	At Pha	W	6-5	Taylor	Raffo	33-27	2	5½
6-20	StL	W	4-3	Ryan	GIBSON	34-27	2	5½
6-21	StL	L	3-5	BRILES	DiLauro	34-28	2	5½
6-22	StL	W	5-1	Gentry	Carlton	35-28	2	5½
6-22	StL	W	1-0	KOOSMAN	Torrez	36-28	2	4½
6-24	Pha	W	2-1	SEAVER	Fryman	37-28	2	5
6-24	Pha	W	5-0	McAndrew	J. Johnson	38-28	2	4½
6-25	Pha	L	5-6(10)	W. Wilson	Taylor	38-29	2	5½
6-26	Pha	L	0-2	G. JACKSON	Cardwell	38-30	2	6½
6-27	Pit	L	1-3	Blass	Koosman	38-31	2	6½
6-28	Pit	L	4-7	Bunning	Gentry	38-32	2	7½
6-29	Pit	W	7-3	SEAVER	Veale	39-32	2	8
6-30	At StL	W	10-2	McANDREW	Briles	40-32	2	7
7-1	At StL	L	1-4	CARLTON	Ryan	40-33	2	7
7-1	At StL	L	5-8	Torrez	DiLauro	40-34	2	7½
7-2	At StL	W	6-4(14)	McGraw	Willis	41-34	2	7½
7-3	At StL	W	8-1	GENTRY	Grant	42-34	2	7½
7-4	At Pit	W	11-6	Seaver	Veale	43-34	2	7½
7-4	At Pit	W	9-2	Cardwell	D. Ellis	44-34	2	7
7-6	At Pit	W	8-7	Taylor	Hartenstein	45-34	2	5
7-8	Chi	W	4-3	KOOSMAN	JENKINS	46-34	2	4
7-9	Chi	W	4-0	SEAVER	Holtzman	47-34	2	3
7-10	Chi	L	2-6	HANDS	Gentry	47-35	2	4

Game No.	Date	Vs.	W-L	Score	Winning Pitcher	Losing Pitcher	Team Record	Pos.	GB
83	7-11	Mtl	L	4-11	Wegener	McAndrew	47-36	2	4
*84	7-13	Mtl	W	4-3	KOOSMAN	Robertson	48-36	2	4½
85	7-13	Mtl	W	9-7	Koonce	McGinn	49-36	2	4½
86	7-14	At Chi	L	0-1	Hands	SEAVER	49-37	2	5½
87	7-15	At Chi	W	5-4	Gentry	Selma	50-37	2	4½
88	7-16	At Chi	W	9-5	Koonce	Jenkins	51-37	2	3½
89	7-18	At Mtl	W	5-2	KOOSMAN	Robertson	52-37	2	3½
90	7-19	At Mtl	L	4-5	STONEMAN	Seaver	52-38	2	3½
*91	7-20	At Mtl	L	2-3	WASLEWSKI	GENTRY	52-39	2	4½
92	7-20	At Mtl	W	4-3(10)	DiLauro	Face	53-39	2	4½
93	7-24	Cin	L	3-4(12)	Ramos	McGraw	53-40	2	5½
94	7-25	Cin	W	4-3	Taylor	Carroll	54-40	2	5½
95	7-26	Cin	W	3-2	SEAVER	Cloninger	55-40	2	4½
96	7-27	Cin	L	3-6	Arrigo	Cardwell	55-41	2	4½
*97	7-30	Hou	L	3-16	D. Wilson	Koosman	55-42	2	4½
98	7-30	Hou	L	5-11	Dierker	Gentry	55-43	2	5
99	7-31	Hou	L	0-2	Griffin	Seaver	55-44	2	6
100	8-1	Atl	W	5-4	Koonce	P. Niekro	56-44	2	6
101	8-2	Atl	W	1-0	McAndrew	R. Reed	57-44	2	6
102	8-3	Atl	W	6-5(11)	Taylor	Raymond	58-44	2	6
103	8-4	At Cin	L	0-1	Maloney	Koosman	58-45	2	7
*104	8-5	At Cin	L	5-8	Nolan	Seaver	58-46	2	8
105	8-5	At Cin	W	10-1	RYAN	Arrigo	59-46	2	7½
106	8-6	At Cin	L	2-3	MERRITT	McANDREW	59-47	2	8½
*107	8-8	At Atl	W	4-1	KOOSMAN	Pappas	60-47	2	7½
108	8-8	At Atl	L	0-1(10)	R. REED	Taylor	60-48	2	8
109	8-9	At Atl	W	5-3	Seaver	Stone	61-48	2	8
110	8-10	At Atl	W	3-0	Cardwell	Britton	62-48	2	7
111	8-11	At Hou	L	0-3	Griffin	McAndrew	62-49	2	7½
112	8-12	At Hou	L	7-8	D. Wilson	Koosman	62-50	2	8½
113	8-13	At Hou	L	2-8	DIERKER	Gentry	62-51	3	9½
*114	8-16	SD	W	2-0	Seaver	Sisk	63-51	3	9
115	8-16	SD	W	2-1	McAndrew	Ross	64-51	2	8½
*116	8-17	SD	W	3-2	KOOSMAN	J. Niekro	65-51	2	7½
117	8-17	SD	W	3-2	Cardwell	Kirby	66-51	2	7½
118	8-19	SF	W	1-0(14)	McGraw	MARICHAL	67-51	2	7½
119	8-20	SF	W	6-0	McANDREW	Perry	68-51	2	6½
120	8-21	SF	L	6-7(11)	McMahon	Taylor	68-52	2	6½
121	8-22	LA	W	5-3	Koosman	Singer	69-52	2	5½
122	8-23	LA	W	3-2	Taylor	Brewer	70-52	2	5½
123	8-24	LA	W	7-4	Koonce	Sutton	71-52	2	5
*124	8-26	At SD	W	8-4	SEAVER	Sisk	72-52	2	3½
125	8-26	At SD	W	3-0	McANDREW	J. Niekro	73-52	2	3
126	8-27	At SD	W	4-1	KOOSMAN	Kirby	74-52	2	2
127	8-29	At SF	L	0-5	MARICHAL	Gentry	74-53	2	3½
128	8-30	At SF	W	3-2(10)	McGraw	PERRY	75-53	2	3½
*129	8-31	At SF	W	8-0	SEAVER	McCormick	76-53	2	3½
130	8-31	At SF	L	2-3(11)	Linzy	McGraw	76-54	2	4
131	9-1	At LA	L	6-10	Bunning	Koosman	76-55	2	4½
132	9-2	At-LA	W	5-4	Gentry	Sutton	77-55	2	5
133	9-3	At LA	L	4-5	Mikkelsen	DiLauro	77-56	2	5
*134	9-5	Pha	W	5-1	SEAVER	G. Jackson	78-56	2	4
135	9-5	Pha	L	2-4	WISE	McAndrew	78-57	2	4½
136	9-6	Pha	W	3-0	Cardwell	J. Johnson	79-57	2	3½
137	9-7	Pha	W	9-3	Ryan	Champion	80-57	2	2½
138	9-8	Chi	W	3-2	KOOSMAN	HANDS	81-57	2	1½
139	9-9	Chi	W	7-1	SEAVER	Jenkins	82-57	2	½
*140	9-10	Mtl	W	3-2(12)	Taylor	Stoneman	83-57	1	+.001
141	9-10	Mtl	W	7-1	RYAN	Reed	84-57	1	+1
142	9-11	Mtl	W	4-0	GENTRY	Robertson	85-57	1	+2
*143	9-12	At Pit	W	1-0	KOOSMAN	Moose	86-57	1	+2
144	9-12	At Pit	W	1-0	Cardwell	D. Ellis	87-57	1	+2½
145	9-13	At Pit	W	5-2	SEAVER	Walker	88-57	1	+3½
146	9-14	At Pit	L	3-5	BLASS	Ryan	88-58	1	+3½
147	9-15	At StL	W	4-3	McGraw	CARLTON	89-58	1	+4½
148	9-17	At Mtl	W	5-0	KOOSMAN	Waslewski	90-58	1	+4
149	9-18	At Mtl	W	2-0	SEAVER	Stoneman	91-58	1	+5
*150	9-19	Pit	L	2-8	VEALE	Ryan	91-59	1	+4½
151	9-19	Pit	L	0-8	WALKER	McAndrew	91-60	1	+4½
152	9-20	Pit	L	0-4	MOOSE	Gentry	91-61	1	+4
*153	9-21	Pit	W	5-3	KOOSMAN	D. Ellis	92-61	1	+4
154	9-21	Pit	W	6-1	CARDWELL	Blass	93-61	1	+4½
155	9-22	StL	W	3-1	SEAVER	Briles	94-61	1	+5
156	9-23	StL	W	3-2(11)	McGraw	GIBSON	95-61	1	+6
157	9-24	StL	W	6-0	GENTRY	Carlton	96-61	1	+6
158	9-26	At Pha	W	5-0	KOOSMAN	Fryman	97-61	1	+7
159	9-27	At Pha	W	1-0	SEAVER	G. Jackson	98-61	1	+8
160	9-28	At Pha	W	2-0	Gentry	J. Johnson	99-61	1	+8
161	10-1	At Chi	W	6-5(12)	Taylor	Selma	100-61	1	+9
162	10-2	At Chi		3-5	Decker	Cardwell	100-62	1	+8

* First game of doubleheader. Complete games in CAPS.

4/8—The expansion Montreal Expos beat the Mets 11–10 on opening day at Shea Stadium.

4/9—Mets beat the Expos 4–2 behind lefty Tug McGraw for their first victory of the season.

4/10—Center fielder Tommie Agee hits two home runs as the Mets beat the Expos 4–2 for the season's second victory. Rookie Gary Gentry is the winning pitcher. The Mets are over the .500 mark for only the second time in their seven-year history.

4/29—The Mets defeat Montreal 2–0 on two home runs by first baseman Ed Kranepool. Jerry Koosman's left shoulder "pops" while pitching to John Bateman, and the southpaw misses almost a month of action.

5/4—The Mets defeat the Cubs 3–2 in both ends of a doubleheader, with Tom Seaver and Tug McGraw picking up complete-game victories. In a preview of things to come, Seaver and the Cubs' Bill Hands exchange brushback pitches, setting the tone for the intense rivalry between the two clubs.

5/14—Left fielder Cleon Jones hits a grand slam off the Braves' George Stone to power the Mets to a 9–1 victory.

5/21—Mets' ace Tom Seaver pitches a 5–0 shutout against the Braves, lifting the team's record to 18–18. It is the latest date in the club's history that they have reached the .500 mark.

5/25—Tom Seaver loses to the Astros 6–3 as Houston completes a three-game sweep of the Mets, outscoring them 18–4.

5/27—Jim McAndrew loses to the Padres 3–2 at Shea for the club's fifth straight defeat. They will not lose again for two weeks.

5/28—The Mets defeat the Padres 1–0, with lefty Tug McGraw picking up the win. It is the start of an 11-game winning streak, the longest in the club's history, and one that will put them in the thick of the pennant race for the first time.

6/3—Tom Seaver defeats the Dodgers 5–2, with Ed Kranepool

blasting two home runs. The Mets record now stands at 24–23. They are over the .500 mark at the latest date in team history.

6/8—Tom Seaver ties Nolan Ryan's club record by striking out 14 in a 3–2 win against the Padres. It is the club's tenth victory in a row.

6/10—Tommie Agee blasts two homers and Cleon Jones one, as the Mets defeat the Giants 9–4 for their 11th straight victory.

6/11—The winning streak comes to an end as Gaylord Perry lifts the Giants to a 7–2 victory over the Mets. But the Mets are six games over .500 and only seven games behind the first place Cubs.

6/15—The Mets lose to the Dodgers 3–2 in Los Angeles; but just before the trading deadline at midnight, the Mets deal Kevin Collins, Steve Renko, Jay Carden and Dave Colon to Montreal for veteran first baseman Donn Clendenon. Clendenon will play a major role in the club's drive to the World Championship.

6/24—The Mets sweep a doubleheader from the Phillies at Shea, moving them to within 4½ games of first place.

6/29—Tom Seaver becomes the winningest pitcher in the team's history with a 7–3 victory over the Pirates. It is his 44th career victory, one more than Al Jackson's 43.

7/6—Donn Clendenon's three-run home run gives the Mets an 8–7 victory over the Pirates. The team is now 45–34, five games behind the first place Cubs. The scene is set for a three-game series against the Cubs at Shea. It is the most important series in the club's history.

7/8—Cub center fielder Don Young misplays two fly balls in the bottom of the ninth, setting up Cleon Jone's two-run double and Ed Kranepool's RBI single, as the Mets post a 4–3 victory over Chicago. Jerry Koosman is the winning pitcher, as the Mets move to within four games of first place.

7/9—Tom Seaver pitches 8⅓ innings of perfect baseball before Jimmy Qualls singles in the ninth. The Mets hold on for a 4–0 victory and are only three games behind the Cubs.

7/10—The Cubs salvage the last game of the series, 6–2. They leave town with the upstart Mets only four games behind.

7/13—The Mets take a doubleheader from the Expos and are now 4 ½ games out of the first. They head for Chicago for the second critical series of the season.

7/14—The Cubs defeat the Mets 1–0 on Billy Williams' sixth-inning RBI single. Tom Seaver is the loser as the Mets drop 5½ games behind Chicago.

7/15—Home runs by Al Weis and Ken Boswell give Gary Gentry a 5–4 victory over the Cubs, as the Mets pull within 4½ of the top.

7/16—Al Weis hits his second homer in as many days as the Mets defeat the Cubs 9–5. In the space of nine days the Mets have taken four of six from Chicago and are only 3½ games behind.

7/20—The Mets split a doubleheader with Montreal, and head into the All-Star break 4½ games out of first.

7/23—Starting left fielder Cleon Jones gets two hits, and Jerry Koosman pitches 1⅔ shutout innings as the National League defeats the American League 9–3 in the All-Star game in Washington.

7/30—The Astros pound the Mets in both ends of a doubleheader, 16–3 and 11–5. In the third inning of the second game, in the midst of a 10-run Astro rally, manager Gil Hodges walks out to left field and takes Cleon Jones out of the game for not hustling.

8/13—The Astros defeat the Mets 8–2 to complete a three-game sweep. Since beating the Cubs four of six in the two crucial series, the Mets have lost 14 of 25 and fall to third place, 9½ games behind Chicago.

8/16—The stretch drive begins. The Mets sweep the Padres 2–0 and 2–1 behind Tom Seaver and Jim McAndrew.

8/17—The Mets take another twinbill from the Padres, this time behind Jerry Koosman and Don Cardwell. They now have a four-game winning streak and move back into second place.

8/24—The Mets defeat the Dodgers at Shea, 7–4. The victory ends a 9–1 homestand in which the Mets cut the Cubs' lead from nine games to five.

9/5—Tom Seaver becomes the first pitcher in Mets history to win 20 games with his 4–1 victory over the Phillies at Shea. Although the Mets drop the second game of the twinbill, they are only 4½ games behind Chicago.

9/6—Don Cardwell and Tug McGraw combine to scatter six hits as the Mets defeat the Phillies 3–0 and pull within 3½ games of the slumping Chicago Cubs.

9/7—Nolan Ryan defeats the Phillies 9–3 at Shea and the Mets are only 2½ games back. At this point the Mets have won 18 of 24 games, while Chicago has lost 10 of 18.

9/8—Jerry Koosman strikes out 13 Cubs, and Tommie Agee homers in the Mets' 3–2 victory over Chicago. They are now only 1½ games out of first.

9/9—Donn Clendenon and Art Shamsky blast homers in Tom Seaver's 7–1 victory over the Cubs. The Mets have swept the two-game series with Chicago and are only ½ game away from the NL East summit. It is also their 82nd victory of the season, assuring the team of its first-ever winning season.

9/10—It happens. The Mets sweep a doubleheader from Montreal, while the Cubs lose 6–2 to the Phillies, and the Amazin' Mets move into first place for the first time in their history.

9/12—The Mets take a 2½ game lead over the Cubs as they sweep a doubleheader from Pittsburgh, 1–0 and 1–0. Winning pitchers Jerry Koosman and Don Cardwell drive in the day's only runs in the first double shutout in the club's history.

9/13—Ron Swoboda belts a grand slam as Tom Seaver wins his 22nd game, a 5–2 triumph over the Pirates. The Mets have now won 10 in a row and are 3½ games ahead of Chicago.

9/15—Steve Carlton of the Cardinals strikes out a major-league-record 19 Mets, but loses 4–3 on a pair of two-run homers by Ron Swoboda. The Mets' lead increases to 4½ games over the Cubs.

✳ 9/20—Pittsburgh's Bob Moose pitches a 4–0 no-hitter against the Mets. The crowd of 38,874 puts the Mets over the two-million mark in attendance for the first time in their history.

9/21—The Mets take a doubleheader from the Pirates at Shea, 5–3 and 6–1, reduce the number for clinching the NL East title to four.

✳ *Shawn, me, Mom, Cindy, Mr. Andušhović, John & John Michael see this game!*

Important Dates

9/22—Tom Seaver beats the Cardinals 3–1 for his 24th victory. The magic number is now three.

9/23—The Mets defeat the Cardinals 3–2 to clinch at least a tie for the NL East flag.

9/24—Before a crowd of 54,928, the Mets get two homers from Donn Clendenon, one from Ed Charles and a four-hit shutout from rookie Gary Gentry to defeat the Cardinals 6–0 and clinch the NL East title. *Mom, Cindy, Shawn & me go to this game.*

9/25—One day after clinching the NL East title, the Mets gather at a Manhattan recording studio to cut an album entitled "The Amazin' Mets." It eventually sells over 50,000 copies.

9/27—Tom Seaver wins his 10th consecutive game and 25th of the season with a 1–0 victory over the Phillies.

9/28—Gary Gentry pitches his second shutout in a row, defeating the Phillies 2–0. In the three-game sweep of Philadelphia, Mets pitching held the Phillies scoreless through 27 innings.

9/29—The Mets post their 100th victory of the season with a 6–5 defeat of the Cubs at Wrigley Field.

9/30—The Mets end the regular season losing to the Cubs 5–2 at Wrigley Field. They finish the season with a 100–62 record.

10/4—In the first regularly scheduled playoff game in National League history, the Mets defeat the Western Division Champion Atlanta Braves 9–5 to take a 1–0 lead in the best-of-five series.

10/5—Two-run homers by Tommie Agee and Cleon Jones (twice) give the Mets an 11–6 victory in the second game of the playoffs.

10/6—The Mets win the first NL championship in their history with a 7–4 victory over the Braves at Shea. Tommie Agee, Wayne Garrett and Ken Boswell homer, and Nolan Ryan turns in seven innings of stellar relief pitching.

10/11—Don Buford leads off with a homer and Mike Cuellar pitches six-hit baseball as the Orioles defeat Tom Seaver and the Mets 4–1 in the first game of the 1969 World Series.

Important Dates

10/12—Donn Clendenon homers, Al Weis drives in the winning run with a single, and Jerry Koosman and Ron Taylor combine to two-hit the Orioles in the Mets' 2–1 victory. The series, now tied at one game apiece, moves to Shea Stadium.

10/14—Tommie Agee puts on a one-man show. After leading off the game with a homer, Agee makes two of the greatest catches in World Series history in the Mets' 5–0 victory. They now lead the Series two-games-to-one.

10/15—Ron Swoboda makes a game-saving catch in the ninth inning to set the stage for J.C. Martin's bunt play that gives the Mets a 2–1 victory over the Orioles. The Amazin's are one victory away from the World Championship.

10/16—The New York Mets, powered by home runs from Donn Clendenon and Al Weis, defeat the Orioles 5–3 on a five-hitter by Jerry Koosman. The Mets are World Champions.

10/17—Gil Hodges is named Manager of the Year by The Associated Press.

10/19—After his spectacular 25–7 season, Tom Seaver is named the winner of the National League Cy Young Award.

10/20—The World Champion New York Mets are given the largest ticker-tape parade in the history of New York City.

INDIVIDUAL BATTING RECORDS

BATTING	G	AB	R	H	2B	3B	HR	RBI	BB	SO	SB-C	GOP	E
Agee	149	565	97	153	23	4	26	76	59	137	12-9	5	5
Boswell	102	362	48	101	14	7	3	32	36	47	7-3	13	18
Charles	61	169	21	35	8	1	3	18	18	31	4-2	6	7
Clendenon													
(t)	110	331	45	82	11	1	16	51	23	94	3-3	9	12
(ny)	72	202	31	51	5	0	12	37	19	62	3-2	3	7
Collins	16	40	1	6	3	0	1	2	3	10	0-0	0	3
Dyer	29	74	5	19	3	1	3	12	4	22	0-0	3	1
Garrett	124	400	38	87	11	3	1	39	40	75	4-2	5	11
Gaspar	118	215	26	49	6	1	1	14	25	19	7-3	1	2
LH	-	139	-	29	5	1	0	11	15	13	-	0	-
RH	-	76	-	20	1	0	1	3	10	6	-	1	-
Gosger	10	15	0	2	2	0	0	1	1	6	0-0	0	0
Grote	113	365	38	92	12	3	6	40	32	59	2-1	11	7
Harrelson	123	395	42	98	11	6	0	24	54	54	1-3	5	19
LH	-	297	-	80	9	4	0	16	44	39	-	3	-
RH	-	98	-	18	2	2	0	8	10	15	-	2	-
Heise	4	10	1	3	1	0	0	0	3	2	0-0	1	0
Jones	137	483	92	164	25	4	12	75	64	60	16-8	11	2
Kranepool	112	353	36	84	9	2	11	49	37	32	3-2	10	6
Martin	66	177	12	37	5	1	4	21	12	32	0-0	6	1
Otis	48	93	6	14	3	1	0	4	6	27	1-0	0	1
Pfeil	62	211	20	49	9	0	0	10	7	27	0-0	5	4
Shamsky	100	303	42	91	9	3	14	47	36	32	1-2	6	2
Swodoba	109	327	38	77	10	2	9	52	43	90	1-1	10	2
Weis	103	247	20	53	9	2	2	23	15	51	3-3	3	13
Cardwell	30	47	3	8	0	0	1	5	0	26	0-0	0	3
DiLauro	23	12	0	0	0	0	0	0	0	9	0-0	0	0
Frisella	3	1	0	0	0	0	0	0	0	0	0-0	0	0
Gentry	35	74	2	6	1	0	0	1	1	52	0-0	0	0
Hudson	1	0	0	0	0	0	0	0	0	0	0-0	0	0
Jackson	9	1	0	0	0	0	0	0	0	0	0-0	0	0
Johnson	2	0	0	0	0	0	0	0	0	0	0-0	0	0
Koonce	40	17	1	4	0	0	0	1	0	7	0-0	0	0
Koosman	32	84	1	4	0	0	0	1	1	46	0-0	2	1
McAndrew	27	37	0	5	1	0	0	3	3	18	0-1	0	0
McGraw	43	24	1	4	1	0	0	3	1	6	0-0	0	2
Rohr	1	0	0	0	0	0	0	0	0	0	0-0	0	0
Ryan	25	29	3	3	0	0	0	2	0	14	0-0	0	1
Seaver	39	91	7	11	3	0	0	6	6	34	1-0	0	0
Taylor	59	4	0	1	0	0	0	0	0	0	0-0	0	0
TOTALS	162	5427	632	1311	184	41	109	598	527	1089	66-40	103	119

1969 NEW YORK METS

INDIVIDUAL PITCHING RECORDS

PITCHING	G	ST	CG	W–L	IP	H	R	ER	BB	SO	HR	SHO	SV	ERA
Cardwell	30	21	4	8–10	152.1	145	63	51	47	60	15	0	0	3.02
DiLauro	23	4	0	1–4	63.2	50	19	17	18	27	4	0	1	2.39
Frisella	3	0	0	0–0	4.2	8	4	4	3	5	1	0	0	7.20
Gentry	35	35	6	13–12	233.2	192	94	89	81	154	24	3	0	3.42
Hudson	1	0	0	0–0	2.	2	1	1	2	3	0	0	0	4.50
Jackson	9	0	0	0–0	11.	18	13	13	4	10	1	0	0	10.64
Johnson	2	0	0	0–0	1.2	1	0	0	1	1	0	0	1	0.00
Koonce	40	0	0	6–3	83.	85	53	46	42	48	8	0	7	4.99
Koosman	32	32	16	17–9	241.	187	66	61	68	180	14	6	0	2.28
McAndrew ...	27	21	4	6–7	135.	112	57	52	44	90	12	2	0	3.47
McGraw	42	4	1	9–3	100.1	89	31	25	47	92	6	0	12	2.25
Rohr	1	0	0	0–0	1.1	5	4	3	1	0	0	0	0	27.00
Ryan	25	10	2	6–3	89.1	60	38	35	53	92	3	0	1	3.54
Seaver	36	35	18	25–7	273.1	202	75	67	82	208	24	5	0	2.21
Taylor	59	0	0	9–4	76.	61	23	23	24	42	7	0	13	2.72
TOTALS	162	162	51	100–62	1468.1	1217	541	487	517	1012	119	•28	35	2.99

• Combined shutouts (12): Cardwell-McGraw 2; McAndrew-McGraw 2; Koosman-Ryan; Koosman-McGraw; DiLauro-McGraw-Taylor; McAndrew-Taylor; Ryan-Cardwell-McGraw; Seaver-Taylor; Gentry-McGraw; Gentry-Ryan-Taylor.

1969 LEAGUE CHAMPIONSHIP SERIES
NATIONAL LEAGUE

NEW YORK METS VS. ATLANTA BRAVES

	R H E	PITCHERS (inn. pit.)	HOME RUNS (men on)	HIGHLIGHTS

New York (East) defeats Atlanta (West) 3 games to 0

GAME 1 - OCTOBER 4

NY E 9 10 1 **Seaver** (7), Taylor (2) SV
ATL W 5 10 2 Niekro (8), Upshaw (1)

Gonzalez, H. Aaron

Aaron's home run off Seaver gives Atlanta a 5-4 lead in the seventh. But in the eighth, the Mets score five runs off Niekro as Garrett doubles past Boyer, Jones loops a single to left, Shamsky singles, Jones steals third when caught off second, Cepeda makes a wild throw home on Kranepool's grounder and Martin pinch hits a two-run single after an intentional pass to Harrelson. The fifth run scores as Gonzalez lets Martin's hit bounce past in center.

GAME 2 - OCTOBER 5

NY E 11 13 1 **Koosman** (4.2), **Taylor** (1.1), McGraw (3) SV
ATL W 6 9 3 Reed (1.2), Doyle (1), Pappas (2.1), Britton (0.1), Upshaw (2.2), Neibauer (1)

Agee (1 on), Boswell (1 on), Jones (1 on)
H. Aaron (2 on)

The Mets pile up an 8-0 lead in four innings, scoring on a double steal and an infield hit in the first, on Agee's homer and a scoring single by Shamsky in the second, on two unearned runs in the third and Boswell's homer in the fourth. Koosman is knocked out in the fifth by Aaron's homer, a walk, Cepeda's double and Boyer's two-run single, all with two out. But with the score 9-6, Taylor and McGraw stifle the Braves while Jones' homer gives New York an extra safety margin in the seventh.

GAME 3 - OCTOBER 6

ATL W 4 8 1 **Jarvis** (4.1), Stone (1), Upshaw (2.2)
NY E 7 14 0 Gentry (2), **Ryan** (7)

H. Aaron (1 on), Cepeda (1 on)
Agee, Boswell (1 on), Garrett (1 on)

After Aaron's homer in the first, Ryan relieves Gentry with two on, none out in the third and a one-ball, two-strike count on Carty. He strikes out Carty, and gets out of the inning. Agee's homer in the third and Boswell's homer in the fourth put the Mets ahead, 3-2, but Cepeda's homer in the fifth makes the score 4-3. But in the Met fifth, Garrett greets reliever Stone with a homer and Jones follows with a double. Boswell's single off Upshaw makes it 6-4 and Ryan keeps command.

Team Totals

		W	AB	H	2B	3B	HR	R	RBI	BA	BB	SO	ERA
NY	E	3	113	37	8	1	6	27	24	.327	10	25	5.00
ATL	W	0	106	27	9	0	5	15	15	.255	11	20	6.92

Individual Batting

NEW YORK (EAST)

	AB	H	2B	3B	HR	R	RBI	BA
T. Agee, of	14	5	1	0	2	4	4	.357
C. Jones, of	14	6	2	0	1	4	4	.429
W. Garrett, 3b	13	5	2	0	1	3	3	.385
A. Shamsky, of	13	7	0	0	0	3	1	.538
K. Boswell, 2b	12	4	0	0	2	4	5	.333
E. Kranepool, 1b	12	3	1	0	0	2	1	.250
J. Grote, c	12	2	1	0	0	3	1	.167
B. Harrelson, ss	11	2	1	1	0	2	3	.182
N. Ryan, p	4	2	0	0	0	1	0	.500
T. Seaver, p	3	0	0	0	0	0	0	.000
J. Martin	2	0	0	0	0	1	0	.000
J. Koosman, p	2	0	0	0	0	0	2	.000
A. Weis, 2b	1	0	0	0	0	0	0	.000
R. Gaspar, of	0	0	0	0	0	0	0	—

Errors: K. Boswell, B. Harrelson
Stolen bases: C. Jones (2), T. Agee (2), W. Garrett

ATLANTA (WEST)

	AB	H	2B	3B	HR	R	RBI	BA
H. Aaron, of	14	5	2	0	3	3	7	.357
T. Gonzalez, of	14	5	1	0	1	4	2	.357
F. Millan, 2b	12	4	1	0	0	2	0	.333
B. Didier, c	11	0	0	0	0	0	0	.000
O. Cepeda, 1b	11	5	2	0	1	2	3	.455
G. Garrido, ss	10	2	0	0	0	0	0	.200
R. Carty, of	10	3	2	0	0	4	0	.300
C. Boyer, 3b	9	1	0	0	0	0	3	.111
P. Niekro, p	3	0	0	0	0	0	0	.000
B. Aspromonte	3	0	0	0	0	0	0	.000
M. Lum, of	2	2	1	0	0	0	2	1.000
P. Jarvis, p	2	0	0	0	0	0	0	.000
G. Stone, p	1	0	0	0	0	0	0	.000
M. Pappas, p	1	0	0	0	0	0	0	.000
F. Alou	1	0	0	0	0	0	0	.000
T. Aaron	1	0	0	0	0	0	0	.000
C. Upshaw, p	1	0	0	0	0	0	0	.000
B. Tillman, c	0	0	0	0	0	0	0	.000
S. Jackson, ss	0	0	0	0	0	0	0	—

Errors: O. Cepeda (2), T. Gonzalez, F. Millan, H. Aaron, C. Boyer
Stolen bases: O. Cepeda

Individual Pitching

NEW YORK (EAST)

	W	L	ERA	IP	H	BB	SO	SV
T. Seaver	1	0	6.43	7	8	3	2	0
N. Ryan	1	0	2.57	7	3	2	7	0
J. Koosman	0	0	11.57	4.2	7	4	5	0
R. Taylor	1	0	0.00	3.1	3	0	4	1
T. McGraw	0	0	0.00	3	1	1	1	1
G. Gentry	0	0	9.00	2	5	1	1	0

ATLANTA (WEST)

	W	L	ERA	IP	H	BB	SO	SV
P. Niekro	0	1	4.50	8	9	4	4	0
C. Upshaw	0	0	2.84	6.1	5	1	4	0
P. Jarvis	0	1	12.46	4.1	10	0	6	0
M. Pappas	0	0	11.57	2.1	4	0	4	0
R. Reed	0	1	21.60	1.2	5	3	3	0
G. Neibauer	0	0	0.00	1	0	0	1	0
P. Doyle	0	0	0.00	1	2	1	3	0
G. Stone	0	0	9.00	1	2	0	0	0
J. Britton	0	0	0.00	0.1	0	1	0	0

1969 WORLD SERIES

NEW YORK METS VS. BALTIMORE ORIOLES

		R H E	PITCHERS (inn. pit.)	HOME RUNS (men on)	HIGHLIGHTS

New York (N.L.) defeats Baltimore (A.L.) 4 games to 1

GAME 1 - OCTOBER 11

		R H E	PITCHERS	HOME RUNS	HIGHLIGHTS
NY	N	1 6 1	Seaver (5), Cardwell (1), Taylor (2)		Buford greets Seaver with a home run on second pitch. With two out in fourth, Hendricks singles, Johnson walks, Belanger singles for a run, Cuellar singles for another and Buford doubles in a third.
BAL	A	4 6 0	Cuellar (9)	Buford	

GAME 2 - OCTOBER 12

		R H E	PITCHERS	HOME RUNS	HIGHLIGHTS
NY	N	2 6 0	Koosman (8.2), Taylor (0.1) SV	Clendenon	Clendenon's homer in fourth is matched in the seventh by the first two Oriole hits: a single by Blair, who steals second, and Brooks Robinson's single with two out. Successive singles by Charles, Grote and Weis with two out make it 2-1 in ninth, and Taylor gets last out after Koosman walks two with two out in bottom half.
BAL	A	1 2 0	McNally (9)		

GAME 3 - OCTOBER 14

		R H E	PITCHERS	HOME RUNS	HIGHLIGHTS
BAL	A	0 4 1	Palmer (6), Leonard (2)		Agee homers in first and Gentry drives in two with two-out double in second. But when Gentry walks three men with two out in seventh, Agee saves three runs with sliding catch in right center as Ryan relieves. Agee saved two runs in fourth with one-hand running catch at left field wall.
NY	N	5 6 0	Gentry (6.2), Ryan (2.1) SV	Agee, Kranepool	

GAME 4 - OCTOBER 15

		R H E	PITCHERS	HOME RUNS	HIGHLIGHTS
BAL	A	1 6 1	Cuellar (7), Watt (2), Hall (0), Richert (0)		Seaver takes 1-0 lead into ninth, thanks to Clendenon's homer in second. But Frank Robinson and Powell single with one out, and Swoboda's diving catch robs Brooks Robinson of a triple but tying run scores. Buford misplays Grote's fly into a double leading off the 10th, and Richert's wild throw to first on Martin's pinch bunt lets winning run score.
NY	N	2 10 1	Seaver (10)	Clendenon	

GAME 5 - OCTOBER 16

		R H E	PITCHERS	HOME RUNS	HIGHLIGHTS
BAL	A	3 5 2	McNally (7), Watt (1)	McNally (1 on), F. Robinson	Third-inning homers by McNally and Frank Robinson give Baltimore 3-0 lead. But Clendenon's homer in sixth, after a pitch nicks Jones' shoe, and Weis' homer in seventh tie it. Doubles by Jones and Swoboda off Watt score winning run in eighth.
NY	N	5 7 0	Koosman (9)	Clendenon (1 on), Weis	

Team Totals

		W	AB	H	2B	3B	HR	R	RBI	BA	BB	SO	ERA
NY	N	4	159	35	8	0	6	15	13	.220	15	35	1.80
BAL	A	1	157	23	1	0	3	9	9	.146	15	28	2.72

Individual Batting

NEW YORK (N.L.)

	AB	H	2B	3B	HR	R	RBI	BA
J. Grote, c	19	4	2	0	0	1	1	.211
C. Jones, of	19	3	1	0	0	2	0	.158
T. Agee, of	18	3	0	0	1	1	1	.167
B. Harrelson, ss	17	3	0	0	0	1	0	.176
R. Swoboda, of	15	6	1	0	0	1	1	.400
E. Charles, 3b	15	2	1	0	0	1	0	.133
D. Clendenon, 1b	14	5	1	0	3	4	4	.357
A. Weis, 2b	11	5	0	0	1	1	3	.455
J. Koosman, p	7	1	1	0	0	0	0	.143
A. Shamsky, of	6	0	0	0	0	0	0	.000
T. Seaver, p	4	0	0	0	0	0	0	.000
E. Kranepool, 1b	4	1	0	0	1	1	1	.250
K. Boswell, 2b	3	1	0	0	0	1	0	.333
G. Gentry, p	3	1	1	0	0	2	3	.333
R. Gaspar, of	2	0	0	0	0	1	0	.000
D. Dyer	1	0	0	0	0	0	0	.000
W. Garrett, 3b	1	0	0	0	0	0	0	.000
J. Martin	0	0	0	0	0	0	0	—

Errors: W. Garrett, A. Weis
Stolen bases: T. Agee

BALTIMORE (A.L.)

	AB	H	2B	3B	HR	R	RBI	BA
D. Buford, of	20	2	1	0	1	1	2	.100
P. Blair, of	20	2	0	0	0	1	0	.100
B. Robinson, 3b	19	1	0	0	0	0	2	.053
B. Powell, 1b	19	5	0	0	0	0	1	.263
D. Johnson, 2b	16	1	0	0	0	1	0	.063
F. Robinson, of	16	3	0	1	2	1	1	.188
M. Belanger, ss	15	3	0	0	0	2	1	.200
E. Hendricks, c	10	1	0	0	0	1	0	.100
Etchebarren, c	6	0	0	0	0	0	0	.000
M. Cuellar, p	5	2	0	0	0	0	1	.400
D. McNally, p	5	1	0	0	1	1	2	.200
J. Palmer, p	2	0	0	0	0	0	0	.000
C. Motton	2	2	0	0	0	0	0	1.000
D. May	1	0	0	0	0	0	0	.000
M. Rettenmund	1	0	0	0	0	0	0	.000
C. Salmon	0	0	0	0	0	0	0	—

Errors: P. Richert, E. Watt, J. Palmer, B. Powell
Stolen bases: P. Blair

Individual Pitching

NEW YORK (N.L.)

	W	L	ERA	IP	H	BB	SO	SV
J. Koosman	2	0	2.04	17.2	7	4	9	0
T. Seaver	1	1	3.00	15	12	3	9	0
G. Gentry	1	0	0.00	6.2	3	5	4	0
R. Taylor	0	0	0.00	2.1	0	1	3	1
N. Ryan	0	0	0.00	2.1	1	2	3	1
D. Cardwell	0	0	0.00	1	0	0	0	0

BALTIMORE (A.L.)

	W	L	ERA	IP	H	BB	SO	SV
D. McNally	0	1	2.81	16	11	5	13	0
M. Cuellar	1	0	1.13	16	13	4	13	0
J. Palmer	0	1	6.00	6	5	4	5	0
E. Watt	0	1	3.00	3	4	0	3	0
D. Leonhard	0	0	4.50	2	1	1	1	0
D. Hall	0	1	—	0.0	1	1	0	0
P. Richert	0	0	—	0.0	0	0	0	0

LOS ANGELES DODGERS, INC.

1000 ELYSIAN PARK AVENUE

LOS ANGELES, CALIFORNIA 90012

TELEPHONE: 225-1411

September 11, 1972

Rev. Larry Vieck
Bridge Committee Chairman
SS Peter and Paul Church
711 Walnut Street
Petersburg, Indiana.

Dear Rev. Fr. Vieck:

There is something beautifully symbolic about a bridge being named in memory of Gil Hodges.

When the Dodgers played in Brooklyn there was no more popular player. When we moved to Los Angeles, Gil built a bridge of his own in winning millions of new fans on the West Coast.

When our team travelled to Japan in 1956, he added to the Goodwill Bridge between our two countries with his play on the field and his generous giving of his off-the-field time to events so important to a trip of that sort.

Gil returned to New York with the Mets and was still "building bridges" as he led his team to an amazing pennant in 1969 and filled the bridges of New York with fans from throughout the area headed for Shea Stadium.

His life span was short but few achieved more than Gil in the important works for his family, his fellow men and God.

My sincerest congratulations to your lasting memory in his behalf.

Sincerely,

Walter F. O'Malley
Chairman of the Board

em

LETTER FROM DODGER OWNER WALTER O'MALLEY TO FATHER VIECK UPON THE DEDICATION OF THE GIL HODGES MEMORIAL BRIDGE IN PETERSBURG, INDIANA.

Special Thanks . . .

The writing of a book such as this one takes the efforts and time of many people. I would like to express my warmest gratitude and thanks to the former big leaguers who played with and for Gil Hodges. Indeed, as most of this book consists of their memories and recollections of Gil, I am grateful they took the time to speak with me about him. Interviewing them, as a writer, was a fascinating and interesting experience. As a baseball fan, meeting and talking to these players was a great thrill. The members of the Brooklyn Dodgers of the Fifties and the 1969 World Champion Mets were my heroes as a youth. They are my heroes still.

I would also like to thank the New York Mets organization for all their help, particularly Director of Public Relations, Jay Horwitz, and team photographer Mark Levine. My thanks also to literary agent Jay Acton for his efforts on my behalf, and Jim Donohue as well. I owe a debt of gratitude and thanks to my editor, Alan Pistorius, who did an absolutely magnificent job, and my publisher, Paul Eriksson, who from our first meeting completely understood my goals for this book. To my business managers, Greg Buttle and Joe Allegro, I'd like to express my appreciation for making my life infinitely easier by taking care of all the "business stuff" thereby allowing me to concentrate on my work.

There are a number of other people who, in one way or another, contributed to the completion of this book, and I would like to thank them as well. They are my beautiful wife Deirdre (who has given new meaning to the word "patience."), my twins Aurelia and Brendan (who at three know the starting line-up of the '55 Brooklyn Dodgers), my parents John and Marie Amoruso, my brother Steve Amoruso; Ames Ressa, who made it possible for me to do this book, Jim and Ann Dick, Jerry and Siobain Berlangero, Wynn and Renee Nathan, David and Robin Klug, Jodie and Chips Monohan, Jim and Laurie Durkin, Dana Nathan, Honey Bodine, Norm Blumenthal, Julie Isaacson, David Wengrod, Frank Coffey, Rosemarie Spera, Karen Blank, Joe Varsalona, Keith Warhola, Charlie Castoro, Diane Dobler, Paul Ruben, Marjorie Hodges Maysent, Dave Johnson, Jon Paloscio, Pat Davis, Leslie Patel, and, of course, my Gordon Setter Jesse, who lay next to my chair during the entire writing of this book.

I will always be grateful to the people of Petersburg, Indiana, who showed me what "Hoosier Hospitality" is all about. In particular I would like to thank Jack Kinman, Bill and Norma Thomas, Bob and Sonny Harris, Bob King, Roma and Eddie Hawkins and Randy Harris. A month after I left Petersburg, the town was devastated by a vicious tornado. Jack Kinman lost his home, as did Bob and Sonny Harris. Shortly after that, Eddie Hawkins, a man whom I knew only a short time, but a man whom I was very happy to have had the privilege of knowing, passed away. His wife Roma is carrying on, as is the town itself. One can't help but admire and respect these people.

Finally, I owe my biggest debt of gratitude, appreciation and thanks to my grandmother, Olimpia Amoruso, my Uncle Ron and Aunt Pauline Heffren, and my cousins Susan, Linda and James Heffren. If not for their patience, understanding, support and encouragement, this book could never have been written. Any success I have had, or will have in the future, is as much theirs as it is mine. They saw me through the toughest of times, and for that I will be forever grateful.

M.A.